herbs

herbs

simple projects for
the weekend gardener

George Carter

photography by Marianne Majerus

RYLAND
PETERS
& SMALL

LONDON NEW YORK

Designer *Luana Gobbo*
Senior editor *Henrietta Heald*
Production *Patricia Harrington*
Art director *Gabriella Le Grazie*
Publishing director *Alison Starling*

Illustrations *Helen Smythe*

This edition first published in the USA in 2004
by Ryland Peters & Small, Inc.
519 Broadway
5th Floor
New York, NY 10012
www.rylandpeters.com
10 9 8 7 6 5 4 3 2

ISBN 1-84172-675-3 (hardback)
ISBN 1-84172-610-9 (paperback)

Library of Congress Cataloging-in-Publication Data

Carter, George, 1948-
  Herbs: simple projects for the weekend gardener /
George Carter ;
photography by Marianne Majerus.
      p. cm.
Includes index.
  1. Herbs. 2. Herb gardening. I. Majerus, Marianne.
II. Title.
  SB351.H5C33 2004
  635'.7--dc21

                                    2003011865

Printed and bound in China.

contents

introduction

gardening with herbs is far more interesting than simply the cultivation of the 20 or so standard kitchen herbs that are so popular. Growing herbs also has an historical fascination because a vast number of these plants were grown in the 16th and 17th centuries for both kitchen and medicinal purposes. Browsing through the early books on herbs, known as herbals, uncovers an exciting and unusual range of plants, with the added interest of association and symbolism. Planting herbs is in fact rather like planting a map of the world because the early herbalists and traders scoured the known world for new species.

Contrary to popular belief, herbs are often vividly colored or with boldly architectural foliage. The projects in this book use a wide variety of herb types, from beautiful Mediterranean herbs in muted colors to more recent introductions with strong colors and foliage variegation.

These herb garden designs range in scale from the very small to the fairly large, but all are possible in an average-sized yard, and many are even suitable for a balcony or window sill.

George Carter

formal herb gardens

Up until the late 19th century, herbs were most commonly grown in formal layouts. One of the classic methods of arranging and cultivating herbs, dating from the 16th and 17th centuries, was the herb knot garden. Other formal plans still in use today include large, geometric beds of a single species of clipped herb, herb topiary, checkerboard designs, and unusual border edgings such as hyssop, rue, and wall germander.

above left An ornamental knot garden containing aquilegias and rose campion, *Lychnis coronaria* 'Alba,' requires a substantial outline of boxwood hedging to avoid a visually confusing effect.

left Old-fashioned cottage-garden flowers such as cream pansies, feathery nigella, and white snow-in-summer infill a boxwood-edged bed.

above The grass path in this beautiful walled garden is lined with lavender and curry plant, both of which grow in loose dome shapes, making their silver-gray foliage useful for softening the edges of borders. Lavender is one of the most aromatic of all herbs. The evergreen curry plant, which has fine silver leaves and yellow flowers, smells of curry after rain.

below Thymes come in many shapes, and in colors ranging from white to crimson-pink and purple. Here, several thyme species have been grown in a small herb garden, revealing the variety of flowers and foliage. The thymes are hedged in by rosemary, boxwood, and a golden form of honeysuckle, *Lonicera nitida* 'Baggessen's Gold,' a shrubby hedge plant.

right An abundance of silver cotton lavender (*Santolina chamaecyparissus*) has been planted within boxwood edging to make a successful and subtle display. Like boxwood, santolina is suitable for use as a divider or edging in formal herb gardens. The yellow flowers should be removed before they are fully developed or the plant will become straggly.

herb topiary

Woody-stemmed herbs trained as decorative topiary specimens for pots and containers add formal structure to an established herb bed or act as a focal point beside an entrance or seat. Rosemary makes a particularly good subject for training into a half-standard. A native of the Mediterranean, it grows well and looks good in terra cotta. You can also train bay laurel or sweet bay and myrtle into topiary half-standards and herbs such as lavender into small topiary balls or short standards.

MATERIALS & EQUIPMENT

1 young pot-grown rosemary (*Rosmarinus officinalis*)

1 terra-cotta pot 11 in (280 mm) in diameter

1 quart (1 liter) potting soil

1 bamboo cane 24 in (600 mm) tall

coated wire or plastic ties

small pruning shears or scissors

1   Choose a rosemary plant with a strong, single leader. Plant in the terra-cotta pot with potting soil. Push the 24 in (600 mm) cane, which marks the final height of the half-standard, into the pot and tie loosely to the single leader using the coated wire or plastic ties. Take care not to damage the bark.

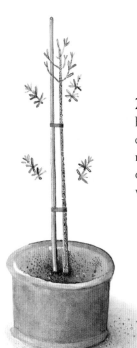

2   Cut off all the side shoots using small hand shears or scissors to direct the plant's energy up the main stem. Leave a sufficient number of shoots at the top of the stem in order to sustain the plant and to encourage vigorous growth in the crown.

3   In the second year, when the stem of the rosemary has reached the required height of 16 in (400 mm) above the level of the soil, cut out the top of the lead shoot. This cut marks the approximate base of the final crown.

4   Allow several top shoots to develop. Once they have reached a length of 3–4 in (80–100 mm), cut out the end of each top shoot. Keep the main stem clear of any side shoots.

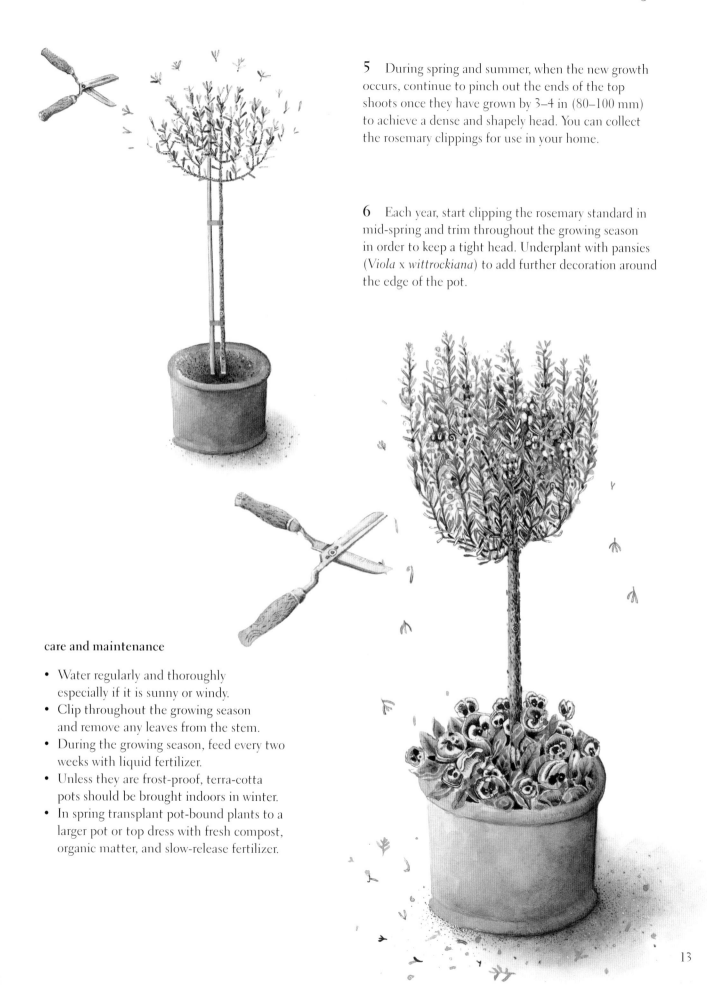

5 During spring and summer, when the new growth occurs, continue to pinch out the ends of the top shoots once they have grown by 3–4 in (80–100 mm) to achieve a dense and shapely head. You can collect the rosemary clippings for use in your home.

6 Each year, start clipping the rosemary standard in mid-spring and trim throughout the growing season in order to keep a tight head. Underplant with pansies (*Viola* x *wittrockiana*) to add further decoration around the edge of the pot.

care and maintenance

- Water regularly and thoroughly especially if it is sunny or windy.
- Clip throughout the growing season and remove any leaves from the stem.
- During the growing season, feed every two weeks with liquid fertilizer.
- Unless they are frost-proof, terra-cotta pots should be brought indoors in winter.
- In spring transplant pot-bound plants to a larger pot or top dress with fresh compost, organic matter, and slow-release fertilizer.

a checkerboard parterre

Achieving a contrast between formality and luxuriant growth is one of
the pleasures of gardening, and this parterre can bring order to an otherwise
informal small garden. The checkerboard effect is based on a design from the
16th and 17th centuries. The herbs are clipped flat and kept square to
accentuate the contrasting colors of the herbs and gravel.

MATERIALS & EQUIPMENT

46 ft (14 m) rough-sawn lumber ¾ x 4½ [1 x 5] (25 x 130 mm)

galvanized nails 2 in (50 mm)

1 quart (1 liter) clear wood preservative

1 quart (1 liter) black wood stain

well-rotted manure

6 squares of landscape fabric 18 x 18 in (450 x 450 mm)

pea gravel

coarse gravel

good-quality topsoil, compost

54 rosemary (*Rosmarinus officinalis*)

1   Cut three 52½ in (1330 mm) and two 70¼ in (1780 mm) boards from the lumber. Cut notches from the boards as shown. The notches should be ¾ in (20 mm) wide and 2½ in (60 mm) deep. Leave a gap of 17 in (430 mm) between each notch.

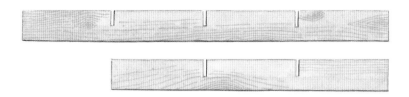

2   Slot the three 52½ in (1330 mm) inner boards into the notches of the two 70¼ in (1780 mm) inner boards to create the inner framework.

3   Cut two 52½ in (1330 mm) outer boards and two 71¾ in (1823 mm) outer boards from the lumber. Nail these four outer boards to the inner framework using 2 in (50 mm) nails. Unless the lumber has been pressure-treated, coat the parterre with wood preservative.

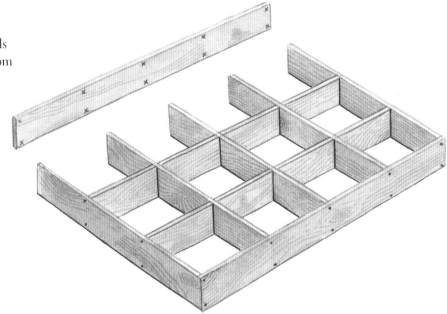

4   Prepare a plot that is about 73 x 54 in (1.8 m x 1.4 m). Remove the soil and create a flat base for the parterre. Plan for 2 in (50mm) of the parterre to remain above soil level. Treat the wood with preservative, followed by black wood stain. With the parterre in position, add the reserved soil to the planting squares, mixing it with plenty of well-rotted manure and extra topsoil, if necessary.

5 Line those squares that are to contain the pea gravel with the 18 in (450 mm) squares of landscape fabric. Fill each of these squares with the pea gravel to 1 in (25 mm) below the top of the parterre. You can vary the effect by using gravel, marble chips, or colored rock.

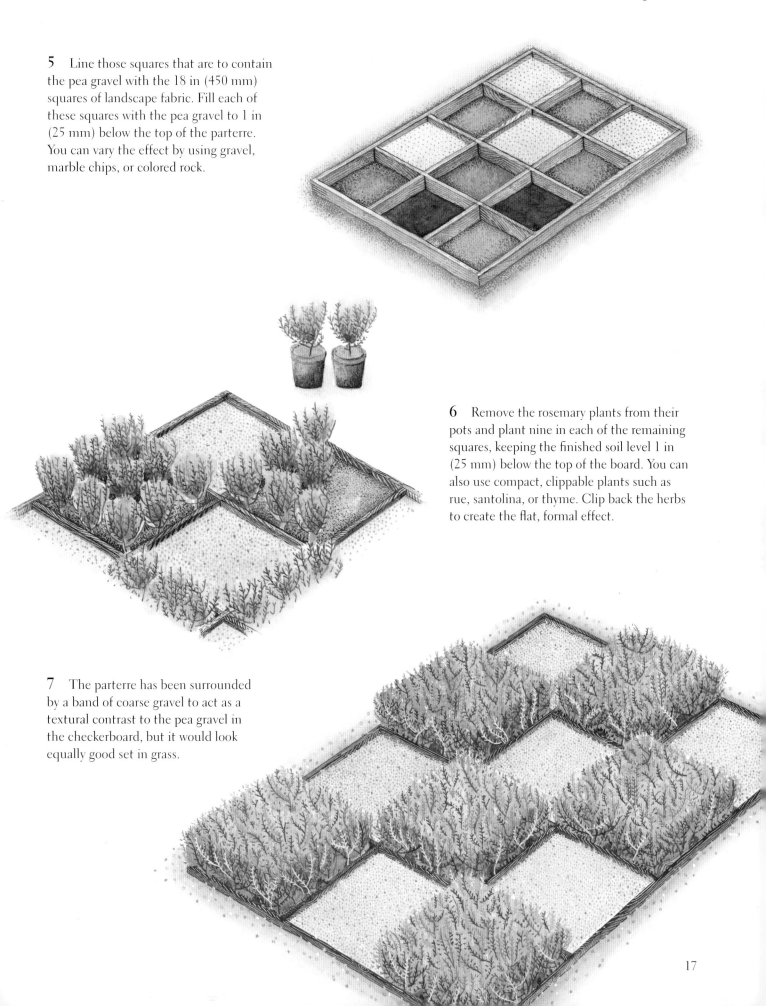

6 Remove the rosemary plants from their pots and plant nine in each of the remaining squares, keeping the finished soil level 1 in (25 mm) below the top of the board. You can also use compact, clippable plants such as rue, santolina, or thyme. Clip back the herbs to create the flat, formal effect.

7 The parterre has been surrounded by a band of coarse gravel to act as a textural contrast to the pea gravel in the checkerboard, but it would look equally good set in grass.

a thyme bed

The large variety of thymes available makes them ideal for collecting, as this bed devoted exclusively to different types of thyme shows. When choosing thyme plants, consider their leaf color, flower color, scent, and habit. Thymes divide into two broad groups—upright and creeping—but in general the tallest thymes will not grow higher than 1 ft (30 cm), making them perfect for confined spaces or under windows. Pot-grown rosemary can be planted at any time of the year, but fall is the best time.

MATERIALS & EQUIPMENT

4 wooden pegs

30 ft (9 m) string

bone meal or root fertilizer

well-rotted manure

15 common boxwood (*Buxus sempervirens*)

19 edging boxwood (*B. sempervirens* 'Suffruticosa')

thymes (see step 5, page 21)

edging spade • square

1   Dig out your bed ready for a fall planting, choosing a sunny location with good drainage—heavy clay soils should be broken up and mixed with humus and concrete sand.

2   Mark out a 10 x 4½ ft (3 x 1.4 m) plot with the wooden pegs and string, using the square to check that the corners are right angles. Remove the turf with the edging spade and dig over the soil (see "Double Digging," page 97).

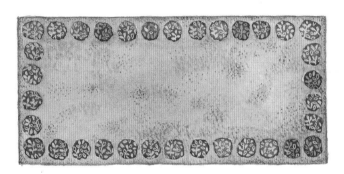

3   Start by putting in a common boxwood in each corner and eleven along the back edge. Then put in eleven edging boxwood along the front edge and four edging boxwood along the shorter sides. The boxwood plants should be planted every 9 in (230 mm) and approximately 4½ in (10 mm) in from the sides of the bed.

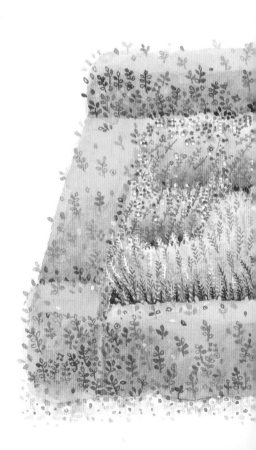

4   Once your boxwood edging has become established, cut it back in spring to encourage new growth and trim regularly in summer to maintain a compact shape. Allow the common boxwood that makes up the back edge and the corners of the bed to grow a little taller.

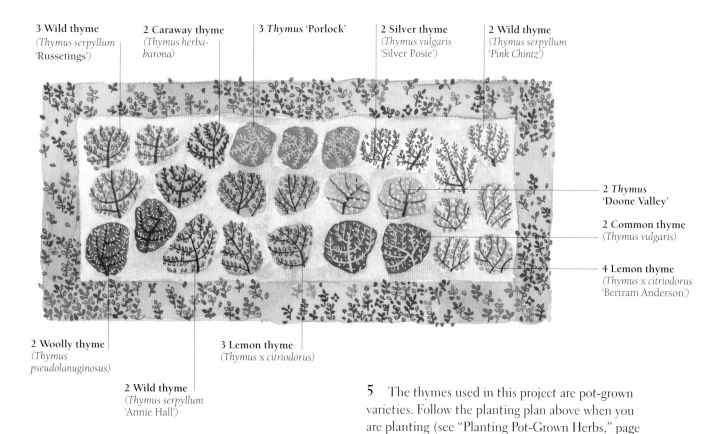

3 Wild thyme
(*Thymus serpyllum*
'Russetings')

2 Caraway thyme
(*Thymus herba-
barona*)

3 *Thymus* 'Porlock'

2 Silver thyme
(*Thymus vulgaris*
'Silver Posie')

2 Wild thyme
(*Thymus serpyllum*
'Pink Chintz')

2 *Thymus*
'Doone Valley'

2 Common thyme
(*Thymus vulgaris*)

4 Lemon thyme
(*Thymus x citriodorus*
'Bertram Anderson')

2 Woolly thyme
(*Thymus
pseudolanuginosus*)

3 Lemon thyme
(*Thymus x citriodorus*)

2 Wild thyme
(*Thymus serpyllum*
'Annie Hall')

5   The thymes used in this project are pot-grown
varieties. Follow the planting plan above when you
are planting (see "Planting Pot-Grown Herbs," page
96). In addition to the varieties suggested above,
there are other thymes to choose from, including
Cilician thyme (*Thymus cilicicus*) and broad-leaved
thyme (*Thymus pulegioides*).

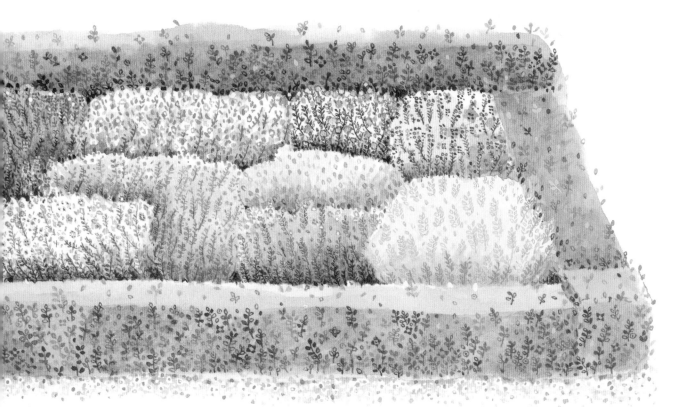

a chamomile seat

Turf seats—consisting of a raised bed made from willow hurdles, bricks, or
lumber planks—have their origins in medieval gardens. Planted with aromatic herbs,
such as chamomile, or mown grass, they provide a pleasantly fragrant and comfortable
seating area. Traditionally the seats were often placed in a niche or in a wooden
arbour festooned with sweet-scented climbers such as honeysuckle and roses. This
described on these pages is stained gray to simulate weather-bleached oak.

MATERIALS & EQUIPMENT

33 ft (9.9 m) rough-sawn lumber ¾ x 5½ in [1 x 6] (25 x 150 mm)

16 ft (2 m) rough-sawn lumber 1½ x 1½ [2 x 2] (50 x 50 mm)

exterior-grade plywood ½ x 17¾ x 45¾ in (10 x 445 x 1145 mm)

4 wood-turned finials 4 in (100 mm) tall with ½ in (12 mm) dowel

no. 8 screws 2 in (50 mm) and 1½ in (35 mm)

1 quart (1 liter) wood preservative

2½ quarts (2½ liters gray wood stain

52 small chamomile plants (*Chamaemelum nobile*)

50 quarts (50 liters) potting soil (approximately)

1 Cut six 18 in (450 mm) side panels from the 1 x 6 (25 x 150 mm) lumber and four 18½ in (470 mm) uprights from the 2 x 2 in (50 x 50 mm) lumber. Drill holes in each corner of the boards, then attach the side boards to the uprights using 2 in (50 mm) screws. Sand the rough edges. The posts will be 2 in (5 mm) longer once you have all the side panels in place.

2 Cut three 48 in (1200 mm) front panels from the 1 x 6 (25 x 150 mm) lumber. Drill holes in each corner of the boards and screw them to the two side panels. Turn the side panels on their sides when you do this in order to make the whole structure more stable.

3 Cut three 48 in (1200 mm) back panels in the same way as the front panels. Drill holes and screw the three back boards to the two side panels. To do this, turn the whole structure over so it rests on the front panels.

4 Cut two 43½ in (1050 mm) battens and two 15 in (350 mm) battens from the 2 x 2 (50 x 50 mm) lumber. Attach the battens to the upper boards of the front, back, and side panels from the inside using the 1½ in (40 mm) screws. Position the battens 4½ in (110 mm) from the top of the upper boards. The battens will provide a good support for the plywood that will eventually form the chamomile seat.

5 Using a power drill with a 1 in (25 mm) spade bit, drill 15 drainage holes in the pieces of plywood, as shown.

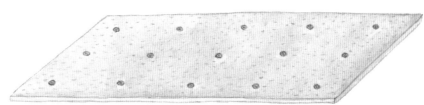

6 Cut a 1¾ x 1¾ in (50 x 50 mm) notch from each corner of the plywood and slide the plywood into position on top of the supports.

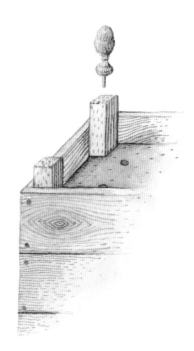

7 Drill a ½ in (10 mm) hole in each of the upright posts and insert the decorative finials. Cover the finished seat with wood preservative and paint it with a gray wood stain.

8 Arrange the plants as shown at right, adding moistened potting soil until the plants and the surrounding soil are just below the edge of the seat. Water regularly and clip when uneven.

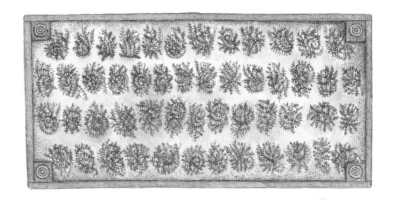

a small knot garden

Knot gardens—with low, interlacing hedges whose function is to divide up beds for herbs—were a popular decorative feature of Renaissance gardens. This simple geometric pattern uses boxwood, but clipped hedges of lavender, wall germander, santolina, or hyssop are equally successful. Colored gravel could also be used in the separate beds to emphasize the design. Preparation of the ground is best done in early fall.

MATERIALS & EQUIPMENT

7 wooden pegs

120 ft (80 m) string

4 bamboo canes

well-rotted manure

160 frost-resistant bricks

weak concrete mix, 6 parts concrete sand to 1 part cement

7 old buckets or containers with drainage holes

95 pot-grown boxwood plants (*Buxus sempervirens*)

1 fully grown boxwood standard (*B. sempervirens*)

pot-grown herbs (see page 29)

edging spade • square

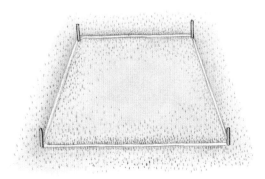

1   Mark out a 15 ft (4.5 m) square plot with four of the wooden pegs and the string, using the square to check that each corner is a right angle. Leave a 3 ft (900 mm) strip of grass around the plot of earth to provide a pathway from which to view the knot garden.

2   Remove the layer of turf from within the plot with the edging spade and dig out the square plot to a depth of about 2½ in (60 mm), removing any weeds. Using the bamboo canes, mark out four lines, a brick and a half in, along each side of the plot. Dig over the soil within the cane boundary (see "Double Digging," page 97). This is best done in early fall.

3   Remove the wooden pegs and string and mortar the outer bricks onto a bed of weak concrete mix outside the cane boundary. Use a weaker concrete mix when mortaring the bricks together. Mortar the upright, inner bricks in the same way. Allow a few days for the edging to set.

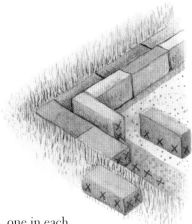

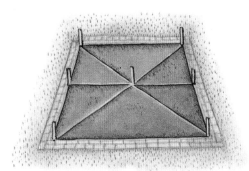

4   Insert four wooden pegs, one in each corner of the knot garden. Insert two more wooden pegs halfway along two parallel sides of the square plot, and finally insert one peg in the center of the plot. Run string between the pegs as shown, to act as a planting guide for the herbs.

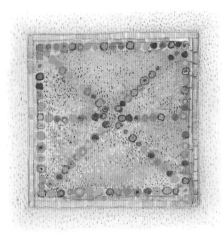

5   Between mid-fall and early spring, put in the boxwood plants every 9 in (230 mm) along the lines of string. Plant the boxwood standard in the center of the plot. The edging will eventually grow around the stem of the boxwood standard. The final height and width of the edging should be kept at about 12 in (300 mm).

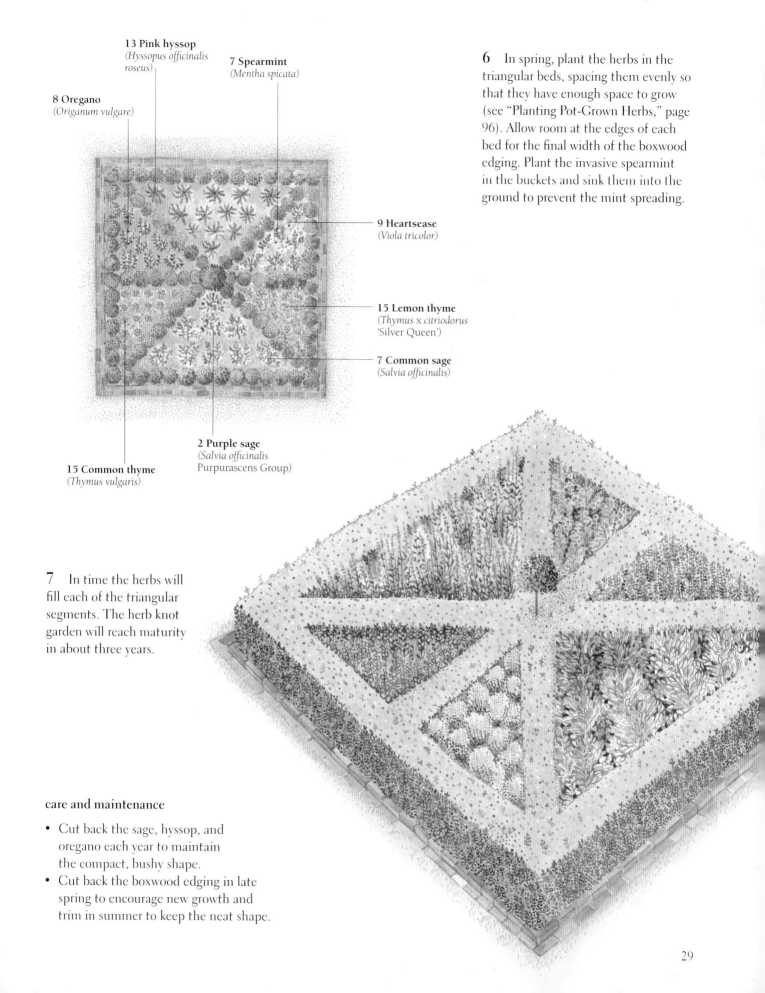

13 Pink hyssop
(*Hyssopus officinalis roseus*)

7 Spearmint
(*Mentha spicata*)

8 Oregano
(*Origanum vulgare*)

9 Heartsease
(*Viola tricolor*)

15 Lemon thyme
(*Thymus x citriodorus* 'Silver Queen')

7 Common sage
(*Salvia officinalis*)

2 Purple sage
(*Salvia officinalis* Purpurascens Group)

15 Common thyme
(*Thymus vulgaris*)

6 In spring, plant the herbs in the triangular beds, spacing them evenly so that they have enough space to grow (see "Planting Pot-Grown Herbs," page 96). Allow room at the edges of each bed for the final width of the boxwood edging. Plant the invasive spearmint in the buckets and sink them into the ground to prevent the mint spreading.

7 In time the herbs will fill each of the triangular segments. The herb knot garden will reach maturity in about three years.

care and maintenance

- Cut back the sage, hyssop, and oregano each year to maintain the compact, bushy shape.
- Cut back the boxwood edging in late spring to encourage new growth and trim in summer to keep the neat shape.

scent and color

Herbs are usually regarded as having a limited color range, but planting plans can make the most of the colors available—such as blues, pinks, purples, mauves, reds, silvers, greens, and yellows—whether from the foliage or flowers. The scent of herbs usually comes from the leaves rather than the flowers. Many fresh herbs, including lavender and rosemary, need to be touched or bruised to release the fragrance, while others smell much better when they have been dried. Take this into account if your aim is to create a scented herb garden.

top Pale lilac and purple lavenders (on the left) and deep-purple thyme (on the right) are particularly fragrant herbs and are also ideal for these simple pots since they prefer a well-drained soil.

above These colorful pinks are planted in a wooden window box. Placed beneath an open window, they are a good way of scenting a room—a device popular among gardeners in the 16th and 17th centuries.

above The rich dark green of boxwood is most often seen as low edging in herb gardens, but the evergreen shrub is also ideal for topiary and can easily be trained into formal shapes to add character to the mixed

bed. In this bed, the boxwood is offset by a scarlet monarda and the mauve of oregano. Monarda, also known as bergamot, provides tall stems of flowers arranged in red, mauve, white, or pink whorls.

above left The gentle colors of lavender and pale purple catmint make them excellent planting partners for a tall, white foxglove. Lavender and roses form the basis of a simple pot-pourri recipe.

left This wooden half-barrel is decorated with shiny lead festoon handles and planted with deep purple lavender and pink scented geraniums.

above This elegant lemon-scented verbena standard has been grown in a terra-cotta pot so that it can be overwintered under glass. Surrounded by a skirt of purple catmint, the verbena's tiny pale lilac to white flowers appear in the summer above pointed, bright green leaves, which smell distinctly of lemons. The dried leaves can also be used as an ingredient in pot-pourris.

a blue and gray border

This mixed border is based on three sections that create a repeating blue
and gray design. A planting plan for one section is given on page 35—plant as
many sections as you like to suit the size of your garden. The best time to plant
pot-grown and bare-rooted shrubs is from late fall to early spring.

MATERIALS & EQUIPMENT

4 wooden pegs

72 ft (22 m) string

2 wooden stakes

bone meal or root fertilizer

well-rotted manure

coated wire or plastic ties

4 pot-grown *Atriplex halimus*

2 pot-grown *Hippophae rhamnoides*

2 pot-grown *Viburnum tinus*

1 *Rosa rubrifolia*

2 pot-grown standard blue holly (*Ilex* x *meserveae* 'Blue Prince')

pot-grown herbs and other herbaceous plants (see page 35)

wooden obelisk (optional)

bamboo cane • edging spade • sledge hammer • tape measure

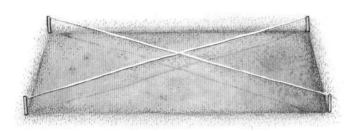

1 Mark out an 26 x 10 ft (8 x 3 m) plot with the pegs. Check that the plot is rectilinear by tying two diagonal strings between the posts. Readjust the corner angles until the diagonals are equal. Remove the turf with an edging spade and dig over the soil (see "Double Digging," page 97).

2 Plant the framework shrubs. For each shrub, dig a hole about twice the width of the root ball and mix the removed soil with well-rotted manure. Put the plant in the hole and use the cane to check that the soil is level, adding or removing soil to adjust the depth. Backfill with the soil and firm in. Water well and top dress with bone meal or root fertilizer.

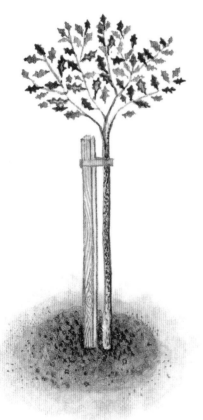

3 To plant each standard holly, prepare a planting hole as described in step 2, then drive a stake into the hole just off-center with the sledge hammer. The stake should reach to just below the head of the shrub after planting. Plant the holly and secure the stem to the stake with a suitable tie. Water well and top dress with bone meal or root fertilizer.

4 In early spring, put in the herbs and herbaceous plants according to the plan below (see "Planting Pot-Grown Herbs," page 96).

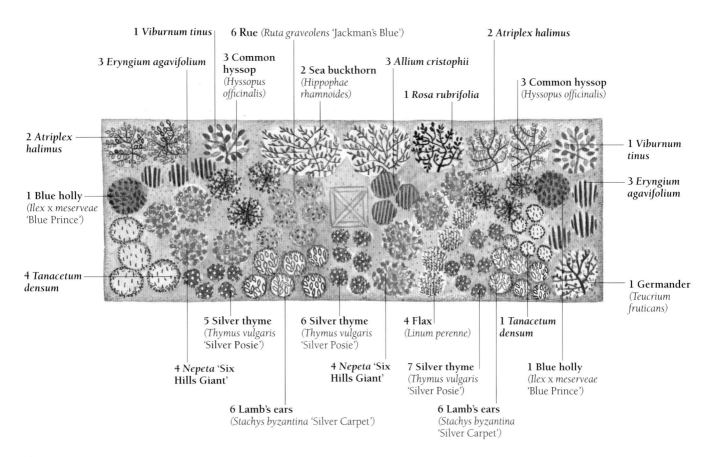

1 *Viburnum tinus*

3 *Eryngium agavifolium*

6 **Rue** (*Ruta graveolens* 'Jackman's Blue')

3 **Common hyssop** (*Hyssopus officinalis*)

2 **Sea buckthorn** (*Hippophae rhamnoides*)

3 *Allium cristophii*

1 *Rosa rubrifolia*

2 *Atriplex halimus*

3 **Common hyssop** (*Hyssopus officinalis*)

2 *Atriplex halimus*

1 **Blue holly** (*Ilex x meserveae* 'Blue Prince')

4 *Tanacetum densum*

1 *Viburnum tinus*

3 *Eryngium agavifolium*

1 **Germander** (*Teucrium fruticans*)

5 **Silver thyme** (*Thymus vulgaris* 'Silver Posie')

6 **Silver thyme** (*Thymus vulgaris* 'Silver Posie')

4 **Flax** (*Linum perenne*)

1 *Tanacetum densum*

1 **Blue holly** (*Ilex x meserveae* 'Blue Prince')

4 *Nepeta* 'Six Hills Giant'

4 *Nepeta* 'Six Hills Giant'

7 **Silver thyme** (*Thymus vulgaris* 'Silver Posie')

6 **Lamb's ears** (*Stachys byzantina* 'Silver Carpet')

6 **Lamb's ears** (*Stachys byzantina* 'Silver Carpet')

5 This border should take approximately four years to reach maturity. A wooden obelisk covered with a climbing rose such as *Rosa* 'Félicité Perpétue' brings added decoration to the center of the border. See Basic Techniques, page 96, for instructions on making an obelisk.

care and maintenance

- Water the border from late spring in the first year if the weather is dry.
- Cut back the sea buckthorn annually to a height of 3–5 ft (90–150 cm).
- Cut back *Nepeta* in fall or early spring.
- Trim the rue in mid-spring to keep a compact shape.

a scented bed

This mixed bed gives a long season of scent and color as well as a good variety of contrasting foliage textures. The bed is both sweet-smelling and useful— several of the plants have culinary uses and many have traditional medicinal purposes. Although this bed has been given specific dimensions, it could easily be adapted to another size or shape of bed or border. The herbs prefer well-drained soil, so pay particular attention to the effectiveness of the drainage. Prepare the bed in fall for a spring planting.

MATERIALS & EQUIPMENT

4 wooden pegs

46 ft (14 m) string

well-rotted manure

pot-grown herbs (see page 38)

edging spade • square • tape measure

1   In fall, mark out a 15 x 7½ ft (4.5 x 2.25 m) bed with pegs and string. Use the square to check that the corners are right angles. Remove the turf with an edging spade and dig over the soil (see "Double Digging," page 97).

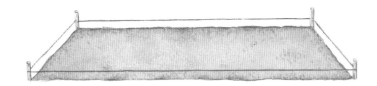

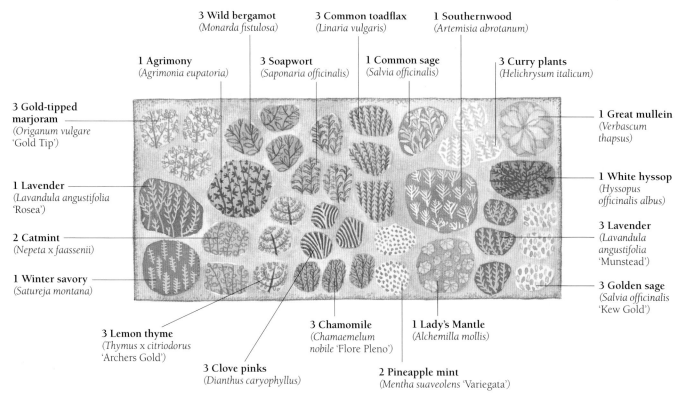

3 Wild bergamot
(*Monarda fistulosa*)

3 Common toadflax
(*Linaria vulgaris*)

1 Southernwood
(*Artemisia abrotanum*)

1 Agrimony
(*Agrimonia eupatoria*)

3 Soapwort
(*Saponaria officinalis*)

1 Common sage
(*Salvia officinalis*)

3 Curry plants
(*Helichrysum italicum*)

3 Gold-tipped marjoram
(*Origanum vulgare* 'Gold Tip')

1 Great mullein
(*Verbascum thapsus*)

1 Lavender
(*Lavandula angustifolia* 'Rosea')

1 White hyssop
(*Hyssopus officinalis albus*)

2 Catmint
(*Nepeta x faassenii*)

3 Lavender
(*Lavandula angustifolia* 'Munstead')

1 Winter savory
(*Satureja montana*)

3 Golden sage
(*Salvia officinalis* 'Kew Gold')

3 Lemon thyme
(*Thymus x citriodorus* 'Archers Gold')

3 Chamomile
(*Chamaemelum nobile* 'Flore Pleno')

1 Lady's Mantle
(*Alchemilla mollis*)

3 Clove pinks
(*Dianthus caryophyllus*)

2 Pineapple mint
(*Mentha suaveolens* 'Variegata')

2   Plant the pot-grown herbs in spring according to the planting plan above (see "Planting Pot-Grown Herbs," page 96). When planting in groups of three, consider the ultimate size of the herbs; smaller plants will need to be closer together than larger ones to create a cohesive clump. Try to avoid a hard planting line by setting the plants at varying distances from the edge of the bed, so that the plants will eventually spill over to different degrees.

3   There are a host of other herbs that produce a scent, activated when they are brushed against. Like the ones illustrated on the planting plan, they can be left outside to scent the garden or picked to be used in the home in pot-pourris. Herbs are very versatile plants and many of the scented and colored herbs featured here, including thyme, winter savory, sage, mint, and bergamot, also have culinary uses.

other herbs with scented leaves

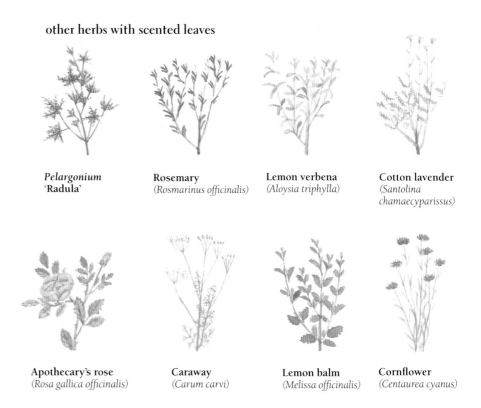

Pelargonium **'Radula'**

Rosemary (*Rosmarinus officinalis*)

Lemon verbena (*Aloysia triphylla*)

Cotton lavender (*Santolina chamaecyparissus*)

Apothecary's rose (*Rosa gallica officinalis*)

Caraway (*Carum carvi*)

Lemon balm (*Melissa officinalis*)

Cornflower (*Centaurea cyanus*)

care and maintenance

- Mullein flowers every other year, so to produce an annual display, you will need two plants that flower alternately. Mullein can be invasive, so weed out excess seedlings.
- Cut back the sage and mint in late fall.
- Trim the lavender in mid-spring.

a purple bed

A purple bed shows clearly that the colors in an herb garden need not be muted
or subtle. Purple is one of the easiest colors to arrange. Many herbs have purple-foliaged
variants. Apart from the purple sage and fennel shown here, you can also choose from
red orache (*Atriplex hortensis* 'Rubra'), purple basil (*Ocimum basilicum* 'Dark Opal'),
and purple houseleek (*Sempervivum tectorum* 'Rich Ruby'). There are also culinary
herbs with purple flowers including thymes, sweet violets, and hyssop.

MATERIALS & EQUIPMENT

4 wooden pegs

16 ft (5 m) string

bone meal or root fertilizer

well-rotted manure

1 pot-grown or bare-rooted rose (*Rosa* 'Roserie de l'Hay')

1 pot-grown dwarf boxwood ball (*Buxus sempervirens* 'Suffruticosa')

3–5 iris bulbs (*Iris* 'Royal Touch')

pot-grown herbs (see pages 41–42)

bamboo canes • square • tape measure

1 Choose an area for your bed, ideally in semi-shade. Mark out a 4 ft (1.2 m) square plot with the pegs and string. Check that the corners are right angles using the square. Remove the turf with the edging spade and dig over the soil (see "Double Digging," page 97).

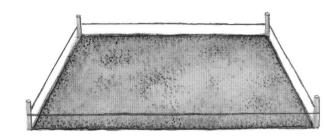

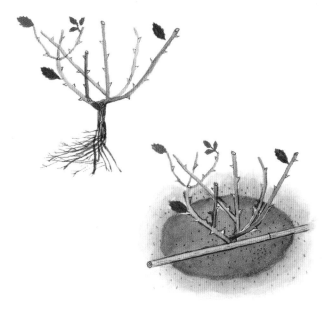

2 Pot-grown boxwood balls and rose bushes can be planted at any time of the year (see the instructions for planting pot-grown shrubs on page 34). Position the shrubs according to the main planting plan. Bare-rooted rose bushes are best planted from late fall to early spring.

3 To plant the rose, dig a hole twice the width of the root ball and mix well-rotted manure into the removed soil. Put the rose in the hole and gently spread out the roots. Rest the bamboo cane across the hole to check that the bud union is 1 in (25 mm) below soil level. Fill in with the removed soil, keeping the plant upright. Carefully tread in the soil and water well, then top dress with root fertilizer or bone meal.

4 Check the position of the irises on the plan. They can all be planted in the same hole. As a general rule, bulbs should be planted at a depth of two or three times their length and two or three bulb widths apart. Make sure your bulbs are healthy and undamaged and place them with the growing point facing up. Gently draw the soil over them and firm in. Water well.

 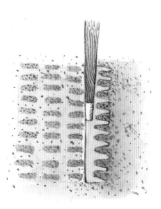

5 Plant the herbs according to the plan on page 43 (see "Planting Pot-Grown Herbs," page 96). You could contain the bed within a brick or gravel border or add a border of slate tiles as shown opposite. A blue fescue in a terra-cotta pot has also been set down near one of the corners to break up the mass of the bed.

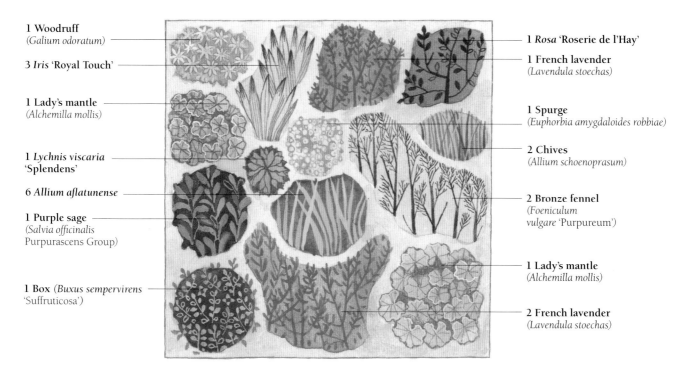

1 Woodruff
(Galium odoratum)

3 Iris 'Royal Touch'

1 Lady's mantle
(Alchemilla mollis)

1 Lychnis viscaria
'Splendens'

6 Allium aflatunense

1 Purple sage
(Salvia officinalis
Purpurascens Group)

1 Box (Buxus sempervirens
'Suffruticosa')

1 Rosa 'Roserie de l'Hay'

1 French lavender
(Lavendula stoechas)

1 Spurge
(Euphorbia amygdaloides robbiae)

2 Chives
(Allium schoenoprasum)

2 Bronze fennel
(Foeniculum
vulgare 'Purpureum')

1 Lady's mantle
(Alchemilla mollis)

2 French lavender
(Lavendula stoechas)

care and maintenance

- Keep all the plants in check in such a small bed to prevent overgrowth and swamping.
- Keep the box to a neat 12 in (300 mm) diameter ball by clipping in late summer.
- Cut back the purple sage in early summer just before the flower spikes develop to keep the foliage compact.
- Dig up the lady's mantle every two years.
- Trim the lavender in mid-spring to control growth.

a raised scented box

This raised window box is best placed below a window, from where the scent and fragrance of the lavender, rosemary, and thyme can drift into the room. You can adjust the height of your stand to suit the position of your window. Choose a window that enjoys a sunny position and keep the plants well watered, particularly in summer.

MATERIALS & EQUIPMENT

1 plywood window box 8 x 8 x 36 in (200 x 200 x 900 mm)

34 ft (11 m) surfaced softwood 3/4 x 1$\frac{1}{2}$ in [1 x 2] (25 x 50 mm)

10 ft (3 m) surfaced softwood 1$\frac{1}{2}$ x 1$\frac{1}{2}$ [2 x 2] (50 x 50 mm)

galvanized finishing nails 1$\frac{1}{2}$ in (40 mm)

no. 8 screws 2 in (50 mm)

1 quart (1 liter) each exterior-grade wood preservative and
exterior-grade latex paint, gray with matt finish

2 strips of $\frac{1}{24}$ in (1 mm) lead, or 26-gauge galvanized
sheet metal 3$\frac{1}{2}$ x 56$\frac{1}{2}$ in (90 x 1450 mm)

2 strips of $\frac{1}{24}$ in (1 mm) lead or 26-gauge galvanized sheet metal 1$\frac{1}{2}$ x 32 in (40 x 800 mm)

galvanized nails $\frac{3}{4}$ in (20 mm)

potting soil

potted herbs (see page 47)

hammer • tin cutters • waterproof carpenter's glue

1 This plywood window box can be bought from a garden center or made at home. If you want to make it yourself, see page 99, where the quantities and measurements of plywood are given.

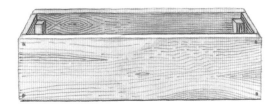

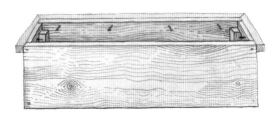

2 For the molding, start by cutting two side pieces 9½ in (230 mm) long and a front piece 39 in (950 mm) long from the 1 x 2 (25 x 25 mm) lumber. Miter one corner on each short piece and both corners on the long one (see page 98). Fit the molding flush with the top of the box; glue and nail from the inside.

3 To make the stand, start by cutting four 37½ in (950 mm) and four 9½ in (250 mm) pieces from the 1 x 2 (25 x 25 mm) lumber. Miter both ends of all the pieces. Glue and nail the joints.

4 Cut four 30 in (750 mm) legs from the 2 x 2 (50 x 50 mm) lumber. Drill holes in the frame corners and screw to the legs. Place one frame ½ in (10 mm) above the top of the legs and another 5 in (130 mm) up from the base.

5 For the lower shelf, cut the following from the 1 x 2 (25 x 25 mm) lumber:
• two 32 in (800 mm) outer slats
• two 36 in (900 mm) inner slats
• three 8 in (200 mm) supports
Position the outer slats flush with the supports and allow the inner slats to protrude by 1½ in (50 mm) at each end. Nail into position.

6 Turn the stand upside down and slide the shelf into the bottom frame. Drill holes for the screws in the shelf supports and screw them to the legs. For added strength, nail into the supports from the outside of the frame. Apply wood preservative to the box, stand, and shelf, and then paint with two coats of latex.

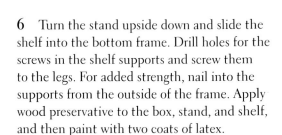

7 Mark a line down the center of one 56½ in (1450 mm) lead strip. Mark two 9½ in (250 mm) long sections at the sides. Divide the side sections into three equal parts and the central section into 10 equal parts. Draw the scallops between these marks so that the top of each scallop meets the bottom edge of the lead. Cut out the pattern with tin cutters. Repeat for the second strip.

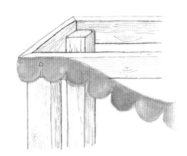

8 Attach one strip to each frame using the ¾ in (20 mm) nails. Put the straight edge flush with the top edge on one side, fold to the front, and use the hammer to form the corners, making them smooth. Nail the second strip to the part of the frame along the shelf.

9 Cut V-shaped notches into the ends of the last two lead strips. Fold over 6 in (150 mm) at each end and bend the central section into a semicircle. Mold to create the wavy effect. Mark three fixing points 1 in (25 mm) below the top molding: one in the center and two 2 in (50 mm) in from the ends. Nail the ribbons to the box, overlapping them where they meet.

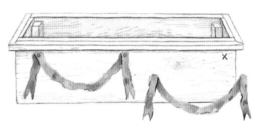

Lavender
(*Lavendula augustifolia* 'Hidcote')

Rosemary
(*Rosmarinus officinalis*)

Lavender
(*Lavendula augustifolia* 'Hidcote')

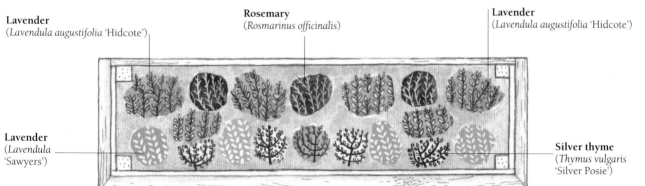

Lavender
(*Lavendula* 'Sawyers')

Silver thyme
(*Thymus vulgaris* 'Silver Posie')

10 Fill the base of the trough with the moistened potting soil. Take the plants out of their pots and position according to the planting plan shown above. Work soil around the plants until the soil sits 1 in (25 mm) below the rim of the trough, then water thoroughly.

The lower shelf can be used to display a row of painted pots of fragrant herbs that complement those in the window box.

an herb drying rack

Drying is an ideal way of preserving the shape, color, and scent of herbs.
Trellis-work makes an excellent drying rack since it allows the air to circulate
around the plants. This project involves a rustic-style trellis rack that provides an
attractive display while the herbs are drying. Choose the herbs shown here or
substitute them with your own combination from the list of suggestions,
and use the dried herbs in pot-pourris to scent your home.

MATERIALS & EQUIPMENT

12 straight branches or stems 5 ft (1.5 m) long

nails 1½ in (35 mm)

3 large galvanized nails

soft string or raffia

brown paper

sealable jars or cans

herbs suitable for drying (see page 50)

1   Make the trellis from branches or stems of hazel, chestnut, or hornbeam. (If you have a suitable tree in your garden, you can encourage the growth of straight twigs by coppicing: in late winter to early spring, cut back the stems on your tree, leaving only the basal head, from which new shoots will grow.) Lay down six branches and position the remaining six across them, spacing evenly. Nail the struts together at the intersections to form a squared pattern. For a more rustic effect, weave in some honeysuckle, wisteria, or clematis.

2   Choose a suitable place for hanging the rack—preferably a dark room that receives no direct sunlight such as a garage or shed. Attach three large galvanized nails to the wall, positioning them so that the top strut of the rack can be hung over them.

3   Harvest the herbs after the dew has dried but before the sun gets hot because hot sun evaporates the essential oils. Pick flowering herbs just as the heads start to open; full-blown flowers do not retain their colors and perfume as well as flowers picked early.

4   Remove damaged leaves and make small bundles of each herb. Fasten the bundles with soft string or raffia using a slip knot—this can easily be tightened when the stems shrink—and make sure you leave a 2½ in (60 mm) loose end for tying the bundles to the rack.

herbs suitable for drying in bunches

Bay (*Laurus nobilis*)
Hops (*Humulus lupus*)
Hyssop (*Hyssopus officinalis*)
English lavender (*Lavandula angustifolia*)
French lavender (*Lavandula stoechas*)
White lavender (*Lavandula* x *intermedia* 'Alba')

Lemon balm (*Melissa officinalis*)
Lemon verbena (*Aloysia triphylla*)
Lovage (*Levisticum officinale*)
Marjoram (*Origanum vulgare*)
Mint (*Mentha*)
Nutmeg (*Myristica fragrans*)
Rosemary (*Rosmarinus officinalis*)
Sage (*Salvia officinalis*)
Savory (*Satureja*)

Southernwood (*Artemisia abrotanum*)
Sweet woodruff (*Galium odoratum*)
Common thyme (*Thymus vulgaris*)
Lemon thyme (*Thymus* x *citriodorus*)
Wild thyme (*Thymus serpyllum*)
Thymus x *citriodorus* 'Fragrantissimus'
Thymus odoratum
Wormwood (*Artemisia absinthium*)
Roman wormwood (*Artemisia pontica*)

5 Hang herbs such as lavender, sage, and bay upside down and arrange them evenly on the trellis rack so that they get plenty of air. Tie in place and hang the rack on the galvanized nails. In a dusty room, protect with brown paper.

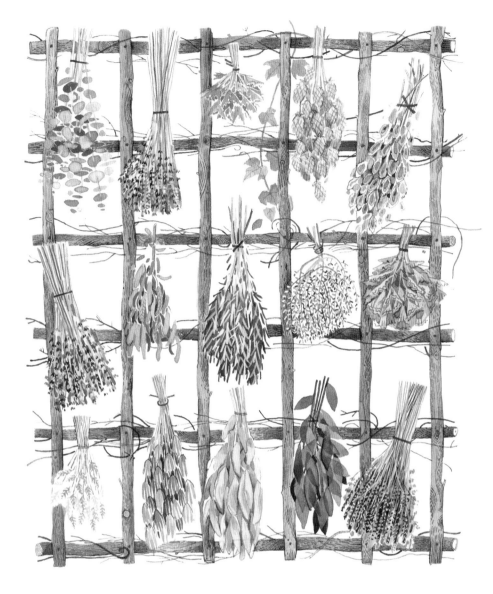

6 When the leaves are crisp and dry, strip them from their stalks and store in airtight containers. Use the loose leaves to make bowls of pot-pourri or aromatic linen bags. In the 16th and 17th centuries, bunches of herbs, such as southernwood and wormwood, were strewn across the floor or placed in drawers and closets to keep away moths.

7 Hang dried herb bouquets from the ceiling to freshen the air and use hop wreaths and festoons as an attractive room decoration.

balcony herb boxes

A roof garden or other small town garden provides a perfect opportunity to grow herbs for purely decorative reasons, although you may wish to combine ornamental herbs with those for culinary use. Even if your outside space consists of no more than a small balcony, these elegant boxes can be filled with color-coordinated herbs to create a gold, silver, and purple display. Either follow the planting plans shown here or devise your own herbal color scheme. These boxes have the advantage of looking decorative both from inside the house and from below.

MATERIALS & EQUIPMENT

4 window boxes 9½ x 7 x 36 in (200 x 200 x 900 mm)

61 in (1530 mm) surfaced softwood ¾ x 1½ in (25 x 25 mm)
for molding (optional)

1 quart (1 liter) each exterior-grade wood preservative,
dark gray primer, and dark green gloss paint

metal vise

hammer or mallet

8 galvanized roofing ties 24 in (600 mm) long

24 roofing bolts 1½ in (40 mm) long with ¼ in (6 mm) diameter

45 quarts (45 liters) potting soil (approximately)

2 plastic pots 5 in (130 mm) in diameter

potted herbs (see page 55)

1 The window boxes in this project can be bought at a garden center. (To make them yourself, see page 99, where exact quantities of wood are given.) Unless the lumber has been pressure-treated, coat each box with wood preservative. Apply a layer of primer followed by a layer of dark green gloss paint.

2 You can also add two 9 in (230 mm) moldings and one 38 in (965 mm) molding cut from ¾ x 1½ in [1 x 2] (25 x 25 mm) lumber. Cut two 11 in (275 mm) pieces and one 39 in (975 mm) piece. See step 2 of the instructions for the window box on page 46 for attaching the molding to the box.

3 The brackets are made from galvanized roofing ties to fit the dimensions of the balcony rail, which in this case measures 2 x 5 in (50 x 130 mm). Mark two 8 in (200 mm) sections, one 5 in (130 mm) section and one 3 in (80 mm) section on each tie.

4 Bend the bracket into the correct sections in the metal vise, as shown, and use the hammer to create right angles. The brackets should fit the balcony rail snugly to make the boxes secure.

5 Paint the brackets with dark gray primer and then with gloss paint. Drill three ¼ in (6 mm) diameter holes in each bracket and bolt the brackets to the outside of the box, securing them from the inside. To make sure the boxes fit back to back along the balcony rail, attach the brackets 4 in (100 mm) in from the ends of two of the boxes and 6 in (150 mm) in from the ends of the other two.

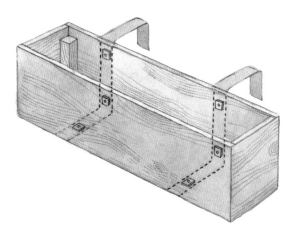

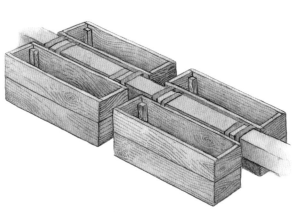

6 Hook the brackets over the balcony rail. The illustration on the left shows how the brackets on the boxes have been deliberately staggered to achieve a snug fit.

7   Fill the balcony boxes with moistened potting soil so that the root ball of each herb sits 1 in (25 mm) below the top of the box. Plant the herbs according to the four illustrations below. Plant the herbs in the larger pots first, adding more potting soil if necessary. Keep the mints, which are invasive, in their plastic nursery pots.

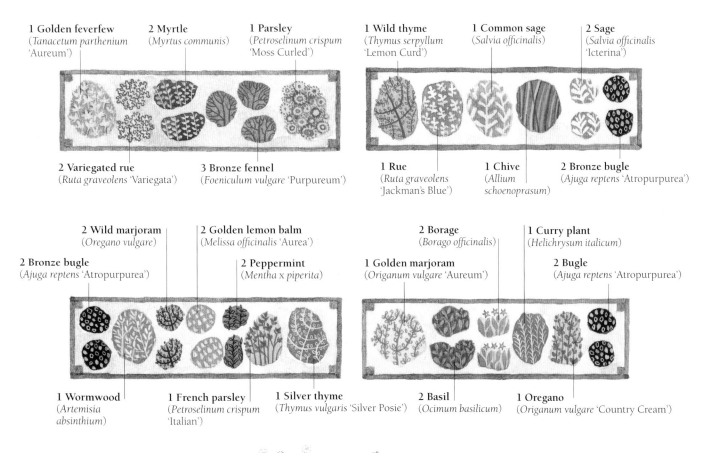

1 Golden feverfew
(*Tanacetum parthenium* 'Aureum')

2 Myrtle
(*Myrtus communis*)

1 Parsley
(*Petroselinum crispum* 'Moss Curled')

2 Variegated rue
(*Ruta graveolens* 'Variegata')

3 Bronze fennel
(*Foeniculum vulgare* 'Purpureum')

1 Wild thyme
(*Thymus serpyllum* 'Lemon Curd')

1 Common sage
(*Salvia officinalis*)

2 Sage
(*Salvia officinalis* 'Icterina')

1 Rue
(*Ruta graveolens* 'Jackman's Blue')

1 Chive
(*Allium schoenoprasum*)

2 Bronze bugle
(*Ajuga reptens* 'Atropurpurea')

2 Wild marjoram
(*Oregano vulgare*)

2 Golden lemon balm
(*Melissa officinalis* 'Aurea')

2 Bronze bugle
(*Ajuga reptens* 'Atropurpurea')

2 Peppermint
(*Mentha x piperita*)

1 Wormwood
(*Artemisia absinthium*)

1 French parsley
(*Petroselinum crispum* 'Italian')

1 Silver thyme
(*Thymus vulgaris* 'Silver Posie')

2 Borage
(*Borago officinalis*)

1 Curry plant
(*Helichrysum italicum*)

1 Golden marjoram
(*Origanum vulgare* 'Aureum')

2 Bugle
(*Ajuga reptens* 'Atropurpurea')

2 Basil
(*Ocimum basilicum*)

1 Oregano
(*Origanum vulgare* 'Country Cream')

care and maintenance

- In late summer to early fall, cut back the wormwood, rue, sage, myrtle, and curry plant.
- Trim and prune all the herbs regularly to prevent them from becoming overgrown.

kitchen herb gardens

Kitchen herb gardens should be planted, where possible, near the kitchen. Include cooking herbs with good colors and interesting foliage in the same way as you would for a purely decorative herb bed, and incorporate some non-culinary herbs.

below The bold architectural foliage of the silver cardoon (*Cynara cardunculus*), which can reach 6 ft (1.8 m) tall, will dominate any herb planting scheme. It looks best, as shown here, against a deep green background of foliage.

above The roots of bay trees tolerate constriction, which makes them ideal long-term container subjects. This bay looks striking in its painted Versailles case.

below Simple combinations are often the most effective. Here golden marjoram edges a bed of rosemary. The stone and brick edging gives the bed further definition.

above left This terra-cotta trough, with its eye-catching swag, shows how easy it is to grow a selection of basic kitchen herbs to decorative effect. The silver and olive-green foliage of the sage, curry plant, and thyme is especially well suited to the rich warm tones of terra cotta.

left This delicate mixed planting contains common mint (*Mentha spicata*) and the vibrant purple and yellow flowers of heartsease or wild pansy (*Viola tricolor*). The flowers of wild pansy can be added to salads or used to decorate sweet dishes, while mint can be used to flavor succulent new potatoes and refreshing summer drinks.

above This basket of cooking herbs is not suitable for long-term planting but it is always useful to have a supply of mint, thyme, chives, and marjoram within reach of the kitchen. After harvesting, the basket can be planted with other cooking herbs.

below A variety of different mints demonstrates the decorative value of herb foliage to good effect. Mints tend to be very invasive, so it is best to confine their roots by putting the plants in plastic pots that are then sunk in the ground.

above A collection of rosemary plants (*Rosmarinus officinalis*) grown in terra-cotta pots makes an arresting display. Rosemary, which originates from the Mediterranean, is an ideal subject for growing in containers. It has the added advantage of being a relatively hardy evergreen, which means that you can enjoy its highly aromatic, needle-like leaves throughout the year. The tiny lilac to purple flowers, which appear from spring to early summer, also provide a dash of color.

right This box-edged knot garden, filled with thyme and sage, is the perfect setting for displaying contrasting textures and colors of herb foliage.

a trellis-enclosed garden

The overall effect of the planting in this enclosed garden is informal, with the herbs growing together to form solid mounds contained by more formal boxwood and lavender edging and trellis fences. The garden comprises four beds of equal size with repeat planting in opposite beds. Plant the herbs in late fall or early spring.

MATERIALS & EQUIPMENT

16 wooden stakes

110 ft (33.5 m) string

bone meal and well-rotted organic matter

4 trellis corner units (see page 98)

16 precast concrete edging slabs 36 x 6 in (900 x 150 mm)

4 wooden obelisks

14 common boxwood (*Buxus sempervirens*)

14 silver boxwood (*B. sempervirens* 'Elegantissima')

4 pot-grown common boxwood pyramids (*B. sempervirens*)

20 English lavender (*Lavandula angustifolia*)

2 pot-grown standard *Phillyrea angustifolia*

2 pot-grown standard honeysuckle (*Lonicera periclymenum*)

gravel

culinary herbs (see planting layout, page 61)

edging spade, square, tape measure

1   Using stakes and string, mark out a plot 15 x 15 ft (4.5 x 4.5 m). Make sure the corners are right angles using the square. Remove the turf with the edging spade and till the soil thoroughly (see page 97). Divide the plot into four beds 6 ft (1.8 m) square with 3 ft (900 mm) between each bed.

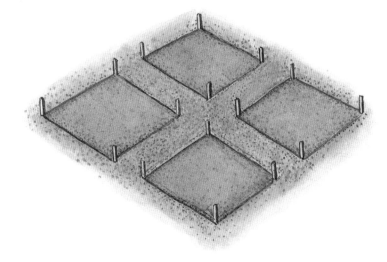

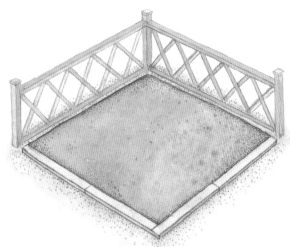

2   Enclose the beds with trellis corner units supported by posts sunk into metal anchors. (Instructions for making the units are given on page 98. A total of 12 posts and 12 post holders will be needed to make four units.) Edge the beds with concrete edging sunk into the ground, as shown, so that 2 in (50 mm) of the edging shows above soil level. Fill the paths between the beds with gravel to allow easy access when harvesting the herbs.

3   Plant seven common box in each bed A every 9 in (230 mm) and five lavender every 10 in (250 mm), as shown. Bed B contains silver box and five lavender. Plant a box pyramid in each bed, one standard *Phillyrea angustifolia* in each bed A, and one honeysuckle in each bed B.

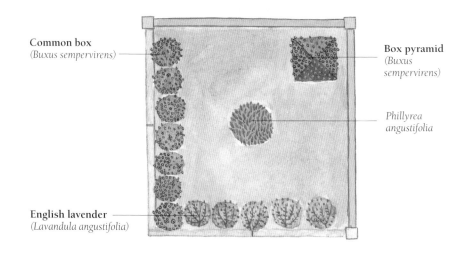

Common box
(*Buxus sempervirens*)

Box pyramid
(*Buxus sempervirens*)

Phillyrea angustifolia

English lavender
(*Lavandula angustifolia*)

4   Buy pot-grown herbs, preferably in 5 in (130 mm) pots. Plant the herbs according to the planting plans for beds A and B shown on page 61, and repeat for the beds diagonally opposite.

5   Cut back the sage, tarragon, and mint in late fall. Trim the rosemary and lavender in mid-spring.

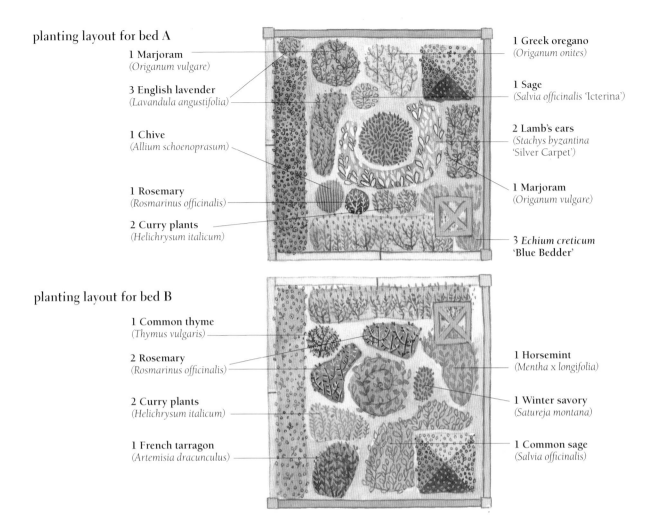

planting layout for bed A

1 Marjoram
(*Origanum vulgare*)

3 English lavender
(*Lavandula angustifolia*)

1 Chive
(*Allium schoenoprasum*)

1 Rosemary
(*Rosmarinus officinalis*)

2 Curry plants
(*Helichrysum italicum*)

1 Greek oregano
(*Origanum onites*)

1 Sage
(*Salvia officinalis* 'Icterina')

2 Lamb's ears
(*Stachys byzantina*
'Silver Carpet')

1 Marjoram
(*Origanum vulgare*)

3 *Echium creticum*
'Blue Bedder'

planting layout for bed B

1 Common thyme
(*Thymus vulgaris*)

2 Rosemary
(*Rosmarinus officinalis*)

2 Curry plants
(*Helichrysum italicum*)

1 French tarragon
(*Artemisia dracunculus*)

1 Horsemint
(*Mentha x longifolia*)

1 Winter savory
(*Satureja montana*)

1 Common sage
(*Salvia officinalis*)

herb staging

This raised herb staging—inspired by the 18th-century staging at the
Villa Pisani near Padua, in Italy, where it is used in greenhouses and in an orangery—
makes it possible to grow a large collection of plants in a confined space. Two sections
of the semicircular design can be used back to back to make circular staging. The
original staging would have been made from oak, but in this project the plywood
used for the curved sections makes a far cheaper substitute.

MATERIALS & EQUIPMENT

15 ft (4.5 m) surfaced softwood 2 x 4 in (50 x 100 mm)

exterior-grade plywood ³/₄ x 24 x 48 in (20 x 600 x 1200 mm)

sabersaw

no. 8 screws 2 in (50 mm) and 4 in (100 mm)

1 quart (1 liter) each exterior-grade wood preservative and

dark green exterior-grade latex paint

9 clay pots 6 in (150 mm) in diameter and 8 clay pots 8 in (200 mm) in diameter

potting soil

pot shards

culinary herbs (see page 65)

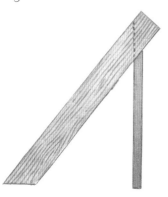

1   To make the front leg, lay a 39 in (1 m) length of lumber on the ground. Using a long rule as a guide, mark out the angles for the cuts by arranging the rule and lumber to achieve the configuration shown. The final length of the front leg should be 35½ in (860 mm).

2   The configuration of the back legs is as shown. Cut two 36 in (900 mm) pieces of lumber and set on the ground as before. Using the ruler as a guide, mark out the angles for the cuts as shown. Note that the back legs butt onto the front leg, so allow for the width of this when marking the angles. The back legs should sit ¾ in (20 mm) down from the top of the ruler.

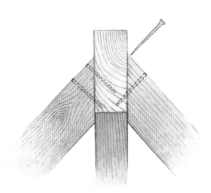

3   Assemble the legs by screwing the two back legs to the front leg using two 4 in (100 mm) screws per leg. Drill the legs as shown. Align the back legs to the front leg ¾ in (20 mm) down from the top of the front leg.

4   Cut nine brackets from the lumber (see page 97 for the bracket template). Position the top shelf brackets first, but cut off a corner from the back leg brackets to a depth of ¾ in (20 mm). Screw the brackets to the legs.

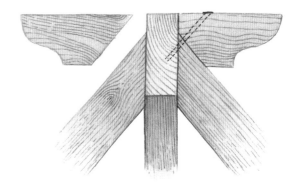

5   Cut out brackets for the middle and lower shelves as before but without cutting off the corners. Position the brackets as shown. On the back legs, from top to bottom, the intervals between the brackets should be 11½ in (290 mm) and 12½ in (320 mm), and the interval between the bottom bracket and the ground should be 10¼ in (260 mm). Drill holes in the brackets and screw to the legs from above. Attach the brackets to the front leg in the same way.

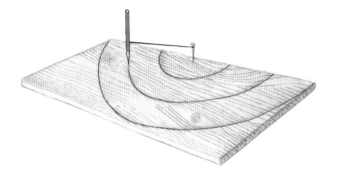

6 To make the shelves, cut from the plywood three concentric semicircles with radiuses of 8 in (200 mm), 16 in (400 mm), and 24 in (600 mm). Mark with a felt-tipped pen attached by string to a nail placed in the center of the long edge of the plywood.

7 Screw the top shelf onto the top brackets from above with three 2 in (50 mm) screws. Attach the lower shelves with two screws per bracket. Unless the wood has been pressure-treated, coat it with wood preservative. Paint with dark green paint.

8 The staging can support nine 6 in (150 mm) pots and eight 8 in (200 mm) pots. Other herbs can be potted up and arranged on the ground. Line each pot with pot shards and pot up the herbs using the potting soil. Leave a gap of ¾ in (20 mm) from soil level to the top of the pot.

upper shelf
• *Nasturtium tropaeolum* 'Alaska'

middle shelf (left to right)
• Wild marjoram (*Origanum vulgare*)
• Sage (*Salvia officinalis* 'Icterina')
• Marjoram (*Origanum vulgare* 'Gold Tip')

lower shelf (left to right)
• Golden marjoram (*Origanum vulgare* 'Aureum')
• Rosemary (*Rosmarinus officinalis*)
• Curly-leaved parsley (*Petroselinum crispum* 'Moss Curled')
• Chives (*Allium schoenoprasum*)
• Pineapple mint (*Mentha suaveolens* 'Variegata')
• Common sage (*Salvia officinalis*)

ground level (left to right)
• Spearmint (*Mentha spicata*)
• Purple sage (*Salvia officinalis* Purpurascens Group)
• Eau de cologne mint (*Mentha x piperita* 'Citratra')
• Heartsease (*Viola tricolor*)
• Summer savory (*Satureja hortensis*)
• Golden lemon thyme (*Thymus x citriodorus* 'Aureus')
• Spearmint (*Mentha spicata*)

an herbal window box

Every kitchen needs a range of basic herbs, and this window box will allow
you to grow cooking herbs even in a very confined space. A symmetrical planting
plan, using a combination of shrubby and trailing herbs as well as a good contrast
of colors, has a more decorative effect. The color scheme here is based on
golden sage, purple basil, and cream oregano, although by choosing
other herbs you can devise your own scheme.

MATERIALS & EQUIPMENT

45 in (1.1 m) surfaced softwood for lattice ¼ x 1⅜ in (6 x 20 mm)

97 in (1.175 m) surfaced softwood for molding ¾ x 1½ in [1 x 2] (30 x 30 mm)

no. 8 screws 2 in (50 mm) and 1½ in (40 mm) long

galvanized finishing nails ¾ in (20 mm)

waterproof carpenter's glue

1 quart (1 liter) each exterior-grade wood preservative and

wood stain (light green/gray color)

pot shards

50 quarts (50 liters) potting soil (approximately)

1 plastic pot

pot-grown herbs (see page 69)

1 The window box can be bought from a garden center or made at home. If you want to make the box yourself, see page 99 for the quantities and measurements of lumber.

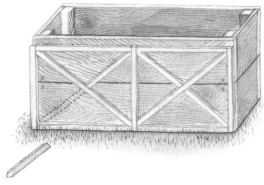

2 To attach the fretwork, cut three 10¼ in (260 mm) vertical battens from the lattice. Glue and nail them to the front of the box so they sit ¾ in (20 mm) from the top of the box. Cut four 13¼ in (360 mm) horizontal battens to fit between the vertical battens.

3 To attach the cross fretwork, cut four 18 in (450 mm) battens from the lattice wood. Hold two of the battens in front of the box on the diagonal, as shown. Mark the pointed angles with a pencil so that the battens will fit within the vertical and horizontal battens. Cut, glue, and nail into place.

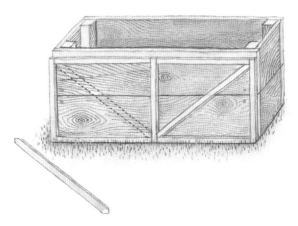

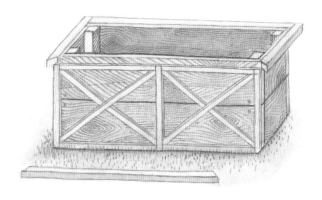

4 To create the crossed pattern, cut two more 18 in (450 mm) battens. Cut them in half, then cut them to fit, as in step 3. Glue, nail, and wipe off any excess glue.

5 To make the moldings, start by cutting four pieces of 1 x 2 (30 x 30 mm) lumber to the following lengths: one 33½ in (840 mm) for the front, one 31 in (780 mm) for the back, and two 12½ in (310 mm) for the sides. Leave the back and one end of the side moldings straight; miter all others (see page 98). Attach from the inside with 2 in (50 mm) screws. Apply wood preservative and let dry before applying the stain.

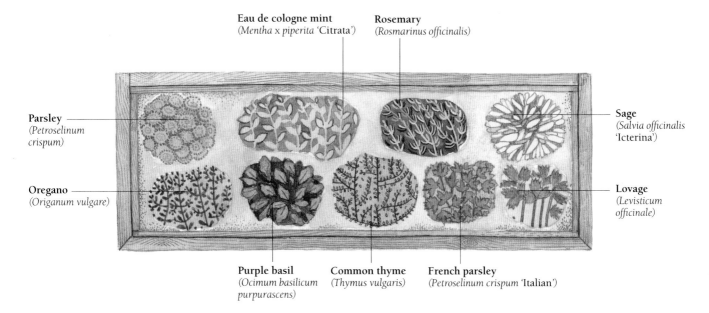

Eau de cologne mint
(*Mentha x piperita 'Citrata'*)

Rosemary
(*Rosmarinus officinalis*)

Parsley
(*Petroselinum crispum*)

Oregano
(*Origanum vulgare*)

Sage
(*Salvia officinalis 'Icterina'*)

Lovage
(*Levisticum officinale*)

Purple basil
(*Ocimum basilicum purpurascens*)

Common thyme
(*Thymus vulgaris*)

French parsley
(*Petroselinum crispum 'Italian'*)

6 When the stain is dry, line the bottom of the window box with pot shards. Take the plants from their pots and tease out the roots. Because mint is aggressive, plant it in the plastic pot, which can be plunged into the soil. Arrange the plants as shown in the illustration and add moistened potting soil until the plants and the surrounding soil are about 1¼ in (40 mm) from the top of the window box.

a small brick-edged herb garden

This narrow herb border can be positioned against the wall of a house, preferably a south-facing wall. It contains basic cooking herbs as well as a selection of scented herbs. The angled brick edging is a simple way of providing a decorative divider between the bed and the adjacent gravel path—a technique that was particularly popular in the 19th century.

MATERIALS & EQUIPMENT

4 wooden stakes

19 ft (5.7 m) mason's line

metal soil tamper

2 80 lb bags ready-to-mix concrete

28 frost-resistant paving bricks (approximately)

coarse gravel

compaction gravel

herbs (see page 73)

well-rotted organic matter

edging spade • mallet • square • tape measure

1　Choose a sunny location with good drainage, preferably against a south-facing wall. Measure out a plot 34 x 80 in (850 x 2000 mm) with stakes and mason's line. Use the square to check that the corners are right angles. Remove any turf with a spade and till the soil thoroughly (see page 97).

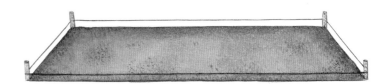

2　The bricks should be laid in the same direction at a 45° angle around three sides of the plot. Dig a trench around the three sides about 6 in (150 mm) deep and 5 in (130 mm) wide. Compact the earth in the trench—a metal soil tamper will do the job well.

3　Mix five parts soft sand to one part cement, make a well in the middle, and add water to form a stiff cohesive paste. Fill the base of the trench about 2½ in (65 mm) deep and set the bricks into the cement bedding. The bricks do not have to be mortared together.

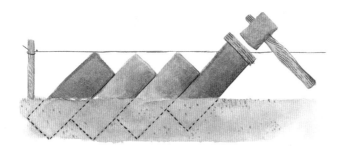

4　Level the edging by setting up a piece of string 5 in (130 mm) above soil level, all the way around the brick-edged bed. Use a mallet to tap the bricks to the required level, but first place a piece of wood between the brick and hammer to protect the side of the bricks.

5　This bed has been edged by a 3 ft (1 m) wide gravel border. After the edging has set, lay 4 in (100 mm) of coarse gravel and top with a 3 in (75 mm) layer of compaction gravel.

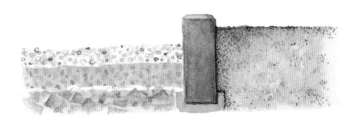

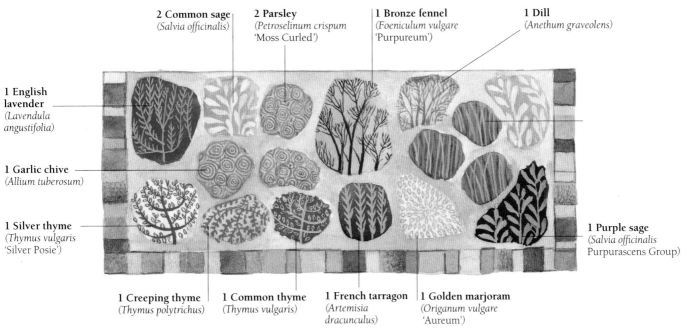

2 Common sage
(*Salvia officinalis*)

2 Parsley
(*Petroselinum crispum* 'Moss Curled')

1 Bronze fennel
(*Foeniculum vulgare* 'Purpureum')

1 Dill
(*Anethum graveolens*)

1 English lavender
(*Lavendula angustifolia*)

1 Garlic chive
(*Allium tuberosum*)

1 Silver thyme
(*Thymus vulgaris* 'Silver Posie')

1 Purple sage
(*Salvia officinalis* Purpurascens Group)

1 Creeping thyme
(*Thymus polytrichus*)

1 Common thyme
(*Thymus vulgaris*)

1 French tarragon
(*Artemisia dracunculus*)

1 Golden marjoram
(*Origanum vulgare* 'Aureum')

6 Plant the herbs in late summer or spring, and avoid planting when there is danger of frost. Arrange the plants according to the illustration above.

kitchen herb half-barrels

These half-barrels are the perfect way to grow a selection of cooking herbs
in even the smallest of gardens, whether you have a small courtyard or simply
a balcony. The planting schemes create attractive displays and provide a source
of fresh produce for the kitchen. Your could also grow other cooking herbs
such as borage, dill, and caraway.

MATERIALS & EQUIPMENT

3 half-barrels, 12 in (300 mm), 19 in (475 mm), and
24 in (600 mm) in diameter

dark gray metal primer

1 quart (1 liter) dark green exterior-grade latex paint

power drill with a spade bit

180 quarts (180 liters) potting soil

1 plastic pot 5 in (130 mm) in diameter

culinary herbs (see pages 76–77)

1 Choose three similar half-barrels with different diameters. Paint the metal hoops that encircle the half-barrels with dark green paint. The paint should remain weatherproof for a fairly long time, but the half-barrels may need repainting from time to time if the paint starts to blister or crack.

2 If there are no drainage holes in the base of the half-barrels, drill three 1 in (25 mm) holes in each barrel using a power drill with a spade bit.

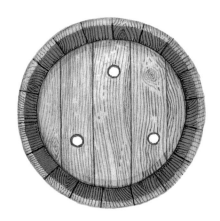

3 Follow the appropriate planting plan for each half-barrel. Remove the herbs from their pots and plant them, adding moistened potting soil to bring the plants about 1 in (25 mm) below the edge of the barrel.

small barrel

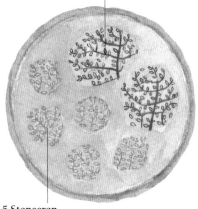

2 Golden thyme
(*Thymus vulgaris aurea*) in 5 in (130 mm) pots

5 Stonecrop
(*Sedum acre*) in 3 in (80 mm) pots

medium barrel

3 Bronze fennel
(*Foeniculum vulgare* 'Purpureum') in 3 in (80 mm) pots

1 Purple sage
(*Salvia officinalis* Purpurascens Group) in a 5 in (130 mm) pot

1 French parsley
(*Carum petroselinum* 'Italian') in a 3 in (80 mm) pot

1 Lemon thyme
(*Thymus x citriodorus* 'Archer's Gold') in a 5 in (130 mm) pot

1 Purple sage
(*Salvia officinalis* Purpurascens Group) in a 5 in (130 mm) pot

1 French parsley
(*Carum petroselinum* 'Italian') in an 3 in (80 mm) pot

1 White thyme
(*Thymus vulgaris albus*) in a 5 in (130 mm) pot

large barrel

1 Gingermint
(*Mentha x gracilis*) in a
5 in (130 mm) pot

1 Chervil
(*Anthriscus cerefolium*) in
a 3 in (80 mm) pot

2 Basil
(*Ocimum basilicum*) in
3 in (80 mm) pots

2 Purple basil
(*Ocimum basilicum
purpurascens*) in
3 in (80 mm) pots

1 Rosemary
(*Rosmarinus officinalis*) in
a 5 in (130 mm) pot

3 Summer savory
(*Satureja hortensis*) in
3 in (80 mm) pots

1 Parsley
(*Carum petroselinum*
'Moss Curled') in a
5 in (130 mm) pot

1 Chive
(*Allium schoenoprasum*)
in a 5 in (130 mm) pot

1 Tangerine sage
(*Salvia elegans*) in a
5 in (130 mm) pot

care and maintenance

- Clip back the purple sage each fall to keep it to a manageable size.
- Replace the biennial parsley once or twice a year to keep it to a manageable size.
- Replace the annual basil every year when the frosts are definitely over.
- Sow chervil twice a year if you want a winter supply.
- Stonecrop needs to be kept dry.

alternative planting

Other herbs can also be planted in the half-barrels, including marigolds (*Calendula officinalis*) and heartsease (*Viola tricolor*) as in the small barrel shown below, and the standard golden bay (*Laurus nobilis* 'Aurea') in the medium barrel. Nasturtiums or hops (*Humulus lupulus*) trained up the bamboo wigwam are an excellent way of bringing height to a display.

informal herb gardens

Informal effects are most easily achieved by planting herbs in large masses. If you allow plants to self-seed at will, they will often produce unexpectedly successful results. By contrast, the finely detailed planting of meadows has an overall pattern rather like an Arts and Crafts design, and should be appreciated at close range. Random growth also looks effective juxtaposed with a geometric border of clipped boxwood.

below White potentilla and purple alliums are fringed by highly scented clove pinks (*Dianthus caryophyllus*) with their blue-gray foliage. The dried flower heads of clove pinks are good in pot-pourris.

left Nothing can equal the freshness of this wild-flower meadow, which is reminiscent of early Italian Renaissance art. Amid the buttercups, clover, and grasses are tall spikes of sorrel (*Rumex acetosa*), distinctive for their small rust-colored flowers. Sorrel leaves are used in the kitchen as a refreshing accompaniment to oily fish.

right This artfully wild border, which merges seamlessly with a gravel path, gives the impression of wonderful abundance. Lady's mantle (*Alchemilla mollis*), alpine strawberry (*Fragaria vesca*), and foxglove (*Digitalis*) have been allowed to grow up through purple sage (*Salvia officinalis* Purpurascens Group) and daisy (*Bellis*) to colonize the gravel.

above These elegant alliums (*Allium cristophii*), with their purple clusters of tiny, star-shaped flowers, look very dramatic in an informal bed.

right The vivid green leaves of fennel (*Foeniculum vulgare*) provide a lush background for flowering herbs such as pinks, cranesbill, and feverfew. The large scale and feathery, open habit of fennel make it an ideal partner for low-growing flowers. It carries yellow flat-headed flowers in summer.

left The sage family is so large that an entire garden could be devoted to different species of the plant. Here, the soft leaves of purple sage and tall, pale lilac and white Turkey sage are set against the delicate flowers of white valerian.

below The elements of this charming gray-and-white bed include white Dutch iris, silver-foliaged artemisia, and *Allium cristophii*.

an informal herb bed

Herbs vary enormously in scale, and some of the larger varieties provide opportunities for creating dramatic displays. This small informal bed, with its bold planting of angelica, tansy, and Turkestan sage, incorporates contrasting sizes, textures, and colors. The bed looks best backed by a hedge, wall, or fence to act as a foil to the architectural herbs, or as part of a semicircular or quadrant-shaped series of beds. It is ideal for a sunny corner in a small garden.

MATERIALS & EQUIPMENT

4 wooden stakes

20 ft (6m) string

pot-grown herbs (see plans A and B, pages 82 and 83)

gravel

well-rotted manure

edging spade

1   Use stakes and string to mark out a 12 x 6 ft (3.7 x 1.8 m) plot that tapers to a 24 in (600 mm) lower edge. Remove the turf with an edging spade and dig the soil thoroughly (see page 97). Remove a further 3 ft (900 mm) width of turf for the gravel edge. You could also surround the bed with paving, but not with grass—it would be impossible to cut with the plants spilling over the edges.

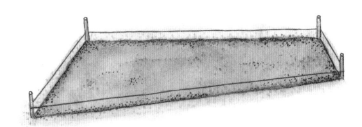

plan A

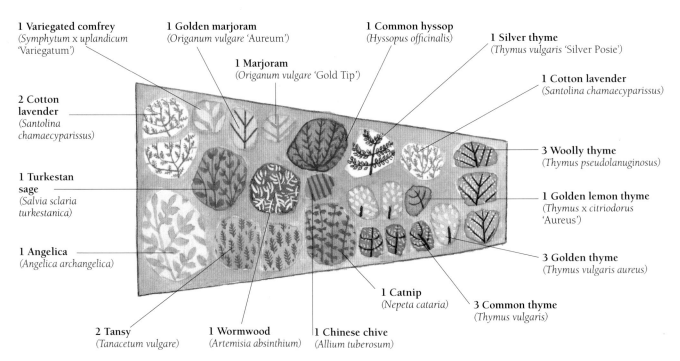

1 Variegated comfrey
(*Symphytum x uplandicum* 'Variegatum')

1 Golden marjoram
(*Origanum vulgare* 'Aureum')

1 Marjoram
(*Origanum vulgare* 'Gold Tip')

1 Common hyssop
(*Hyssopus officinalis*)

1 Silver thyme
(*Thymus vulgaris* 'Silver Posie')

2 Cotton lavender
(*Santolina chamaecyparissus*)

1 Cotton lavender
(*Santolina chamaecyparissus*)

3 Woolly thyme
(*Thymus pseudolanuginosus*)

1 Turkestan sage
(*Salvia sclaria turkestanica*)

1 Golden lemon thyme
(*Thymus x citriodorus* 'Aureus')

1 Angelica
(*Angelica archangelica*)

3 Golden thyme
(*Thymus vulgaris aureus*)

2 Tansy
(*Tanacetum vulgare*)

1 Wormwood
(*Artemisia absinthium*)

1 Chinese chive
(*Allium tuberosum*)

1 Catnip
(*Nepeta cataria*)

3 Common thyme
(*Thymus vulgaris*)

2   The herbs used in this project prefer a warm, sunny site and well-drained soil. They are all perennials or shrubs except for the biennial angelica. Allium is a bulb. Follow the planting plan when putting in the herbs. The best time to plant the bed is in mid-fall or mid-spring.

3   This wedge-shaped bed looks good alone but it can also be repeated to make a more complex design such as a semicircular or a quadrant-shaped garden. To create a more varied effect, alternate the herbs using the planting plan below.

plan B

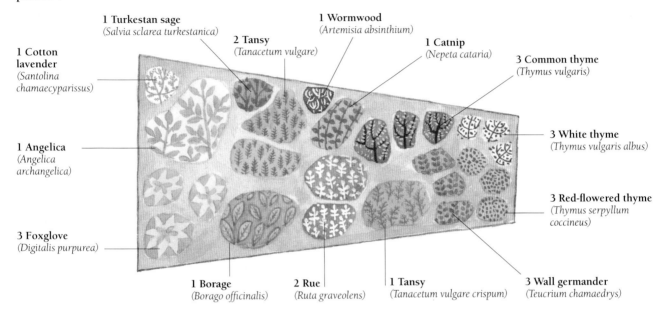

1 Cotton lavender
(*Santolina chamaecyparissus*)

1 Turkestan sage
(*Salvia sclarea turkestanica*)

2 Tansy
(*Tanacetum vulgare*)

1 Wormwood
(*Artemisia absinthium*)

1 Catnip
(*Nepeta cataria*)

3 Common thyme
(*Thymus vulgaris*)

1 Angelica
(*Angelica archangelica*)

3 White thyme
(*Thymus vulgaris albus*)

3 Red-flowered thyme
(*Thymus serpyllum coccineus*)

3 Foxglove
(*Digitalis purpurea*)

1 Borage
(*Borago officinalis*)

2 Rue
(*Ruta graveolens*)

1 Tansy
(*Tanacetum vulgare crispum*)

3 Wall germander
(*Teucrium chamaedrys*)

care and maintenance

- Allow the herbs to spill out over the edge of the bed. If you are using a gravel surround, allow it to encroach into the bed.
- Clip the cotton lavender during the summer to maintain a compact shape.

- Remove all dead growth in early spring.
- Allow the biennial angelica to self-seed but weed out any germinating seedlings.
- During the winter cut back old or dead growth that lies over other plants, but retain excess growth where possible to act as frost protection.

a flowery mead

The composition of a wildflower meadow or mead needs to be carefully planned
in relation to the soil type, aspect, and conditions of your site. You should aim to achieve
a balance of plants that can coexist without one species becoming dominant. Although
wildflower mixes are available, it is more fun to put together your own mixture of plants.
A wildflower meadow need not be large although it can take up as much space as
you wish. This project measures 14 x 18 ft (4.3 x 5.6 m) and is suitable for a city
garden. The site should be prepared well in advance of planting.

MATERIALS & EQUIPMENT

4 stakes

65 ft (20 m) string

lightly colored sand

128 hawthorn (*Crataegus mongyna*)

3 oz (85 g) mixed grasses (see page 86)

3.75 oz (106 g) mixed wildflowers (see page 86)

bag

pieces of stiff foil or thin cardboard

fork • rake • set of scales • square

1   Choose a sunny, well-drained site for this wildflower mix. The seed can be sown in fall or spring but the preparation should be done well in advance. Use stakes and string to mark out a 14 x 18 ft (4.3 x 5.6 m) plot. Use a square to check that the corners are right angles.

2   Remove the turf with a spade and dig over the soil with a fork, removing any weeds or weed roots. Avoid digging down too deep and raising any weed seeds. Break up the surface to a fine tilth and rake flat.

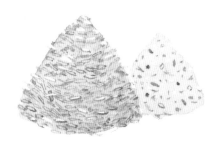

3   The seed is mixed in the ratio of 80 per cent grass seed to 20 per cent wildflower seed. In a small area you may want to increase the ratio of flowers to grass for more color, although this may undermine the natural meadow effect. Weigh out the correct amount of seed, dividing the amounts by the number of plant species so that you achieve a balanced mix. Mix the seed in a bag.

flowers

Bird's foot trefoil
Common knapweed
Greater knapweed
Musk mallow
Yarrow
Yellow rattle

grasses

Cocksfoot
Common bent
Red fescue

other possible flowers

Common veitch
Cow parsley
Cowslip
Field scabious
Goat's beard
Meadow clary
Meadow cranesbill
Ox-eye daisy
Red clover
Rough hawkbit
Sorrel
White clover
White deadnettle
Wild parsley

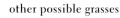

other possible grasses

Meadow foxtail
Smooth meadow grass
Sweet venal grass
Rye grass
Yellow oat grass

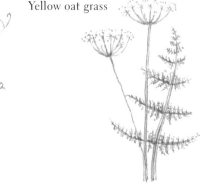

4   Divide the site into 24 in (600 mm) squares with the lightly colored sand. Sow in spring in very cold areas, and in the fall in hot, dry areas so that the plants can become established before drought conditions set in. Divide the bag of seed into roughly equal portions and sprinkle in one portion of seed into each square. Rake in the seed and lightly firm in with your feet.

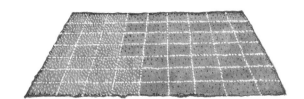

5   Protect the seed from birds by setting up a simple bird scarer. String stretched between wooden stakes 6 in (150 mm) above ground level is ideal. Tie stiff foil or thin card to the string at 36 in (900 mm) intervals to act as a deterrent.

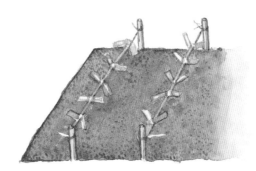

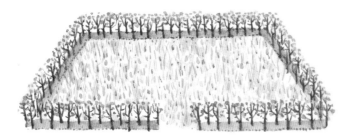

6   A low hawthorn hedge reinforces the rural atmosphere and separates the meadow from more formal parts of the garden. Hawthorn is fast-growing and will require frequent clipping to keep it to shape. Prepare a 12 in (300 mm) wide trench around the meadow. Plant the hawthorn plants every 12 in (300 mm) in double staggered rows, as shown, to create a dense hedge.

7   It will take several years for the equilibrium of the meadow to settle down. If the mix contains no spring-flowering plants keep the meadow cut to a height of 2 in (50 mm) until late spring, then leave uncut until the end of the main summer flowering season, which will last about one month.

care and maintenance

- Weed out extraneous plants that are not part of your original design. Make sure you know what your wild flowers look like so that you can identify the weeds.
- Cut down the grass and flowers to a height of 2 in (50 mm) in the first year with a lawnmower so that the more vigorous plants do not become over-established at the expense of the others.

- Cut down vigorous grasses and flowers when they reach 2¾ in (70 mm).
- Water the seedlings in a very dry early growing season, soaking them thoroughly so that the water penetrates deep into the soil.
- After the main flowering season, cut back to 3–4 in (80–100 mm) at least once a month.

an herb-lined pathway

A brick or paved pathway makes an herb garden accessible even in wet or muddy weather. Paths also articulate and define a design, fulfilling much the same role as dwarf hedges or grass edging. You do not need much space to make this type of pathway. The herb bed included in this project, which measures only 5 x 6 ft (1.5 x 1.8 m), will fit even the tiniest of gardens. The herbs should be allowed to flow informally over edges of the path.

MATERIALS & EQUIPMENT

4 wooden stakes

23 ft (7 m) string

well-rotted organic matter

1 concrete paver 2 x 2 ft (600 x 600 mm)

9 SW (frost-resistant) bricks

metal soil tamper

gravel

sand

landscape fabric

5 plastic pots or buckets

1 terra-cotta pot 12 in (300 mm) in diameter

herbs (see pages 91)

edging spade • level • square • tape measure

1   Dig your bed ready for a fall or spring planting, choosing a spot in full sun or part shade. Mark out a 5 x 6 ft (1.5 x 1.8 m) plot with wooden stakes and string, using the square to make sure the corners are right angles. Remove the turf with the edging spade and till the soil thoroughly (see page 97). Amend the soil with well-rotted manure.

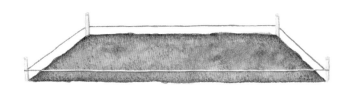

2   The bricks used here are high-fired engineering bricks (although any paving brick is suitable). Their purplish color works well with the purple sage in the planting. To lay the brick paving and concrete paver, dig out an 8 in (250 mm) wide trench to a depth of 6 in (150 mm). Make a 24 in (600 mm) square for the paver. (See opposite for path and paver layout.)

3   Compress the soil in the trench with a soil tamper or use your feet; this will make a solid base for the bricks and the paver.

4   Spread a 4 in (100 mm) layer of gravel in the trench. Top this with landscape fabric. Then spread 2 in (50 mm) of sand. Tamp the sand and spray lightly with water. Gently position the bricks and the paver. Use the level to make sure they are level as you go.

6   Try to buy good-sized herbs that have been grown in 4 in (100 mm) pots; the summer savory and bay can be bought in 6 in (150 mm) pots. Plant the herbs in fall or spring according to the planting plan on page 91. Plant the mints in buckets or pots then sink them into the ground because mint is invasive. Plant the golden lemon balm in a 12 in (300 mm) clay pot to make a focal point in the center of the bed.

5   Before starting to plant, incorporate some gravel where you plant the thyme if your soil is not free-draining.

3 Variegated gingermint
(*Mentha* x *gracilis* 'Variegata')

2 Wild strawberry
(*Fragaria vesca*)

1 Golden lemon balm
(*Melissa officinalis* 'Aurea')

1 Bay
(*Laurus nobilis*)

2 Golden marjoram
(*Origanum vulgare* 'Aureum')

2 Variegated gingermint
(*Mentha* x *gracilis* 'Variegata')

4 Lemon thyme
(*Thymus* x *citriodorus* 'Bertram Anderson')

2 Wild strawberry
(*Fragaria vesca*)

1 Summer savory
(*Satureja hortensis*)

2 Golden marjoram
(*Origanum vulgare* 'Aureum')

2 Oregano
(*Origanum vulgare*)

1 Bay
(*Laurus nobilis*)

1 Summer savory
(*Satureja hortensis*)

3 Purple sage
(*Salvia officinalis* Purpurascens Group)

4 Lemon thyme
(*Thymus* x *citriodorus* 'Bertram Anderson')

care and maintenance

- Trim back the herbs when necessary to prevent them crowding one other.
- Cut back new growth on the bay in early summer.
- Cut back the sage before it flowers to achieve a compact shape.
- Trim the thyme after flowering to encourage bushy growth.

herbs with architectural foliage

This bed breaks with the convention that dictates that there should be small plants in the foreground of a composition. Tall plants are scattered throughout to produce an imposing mass of foliage, with smaller plants showing through here and there. Even in very small gardens, a large-scale bed can be dramatically successful, creating a lush, jungle-like effect.

MATERIALS & EQUIPMENT

4 wooden stakes

62 ft (19 m) string

bone meal or root fertilizer

well-rotted manure

2 southernwood (*Artemisia abrotanum*)

1 *Buddleia davidii*

1 *Rosa* 'Madame Isaac Pereire'

1 *Rosa* 'Chapeau de Napoleon'

pot-grown herbs and herbaceous plants (see page 95)

wooden obelisk (optional)

edging spade • square • tape measure

1   Dig out the bed in fall. Choose a sunny location with good drainage—heavy clays should be broken up and mixed with humus and concrete sand. Mark out a 12 x 18 ft (3.7 x 5.5 m) plot with stakes and string and use a square to check that the corners are right angles. Remove the turf with an edging spade and dig the soil thoroughly (see page 97).

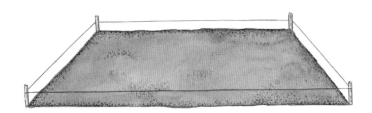

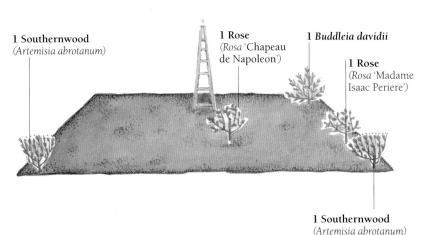

1 Southernwood
(Artemisia abrotanum)

1 Rose
(Rosa 'Chapeau de Napoleon')

1 *Buddleia davidii*

1 Rose
(Rosa 'Madame Isaac Periere')

1 Southernwood
(Artemisia abrotanum)

2   The best time to plant bare-rooted shrubs is from late fall to early spring. Dig a hole large enough to accommodate the roots without cramping them and mix the removed soil with well-rotted manure. For the roses ensure that the union is about 1 in (25 mm) below soil level.

3   Backfill with the removed soil and firm in. Water well and top dress with bone meal or root fertilizer. To make an obelisk, see instructions on page 96.

alternative architectural herbs

Hops
(Humulus lupulus)

Dill
(Anethum graveolens)

Mondo grass
(Ophiopogon japonicus)

Queen Anne's lace
(Ammi majus)

Common horseradish
(Armorachia rusticana)

Red orache
(Atriplex hortensis 'Rubra')

care and maintenance

- Prune the roses during late winter or early spring. Reduce long new shoots. Dead-head from early summer.
- Dead-head the *Tanacetum parthenium* 'Aureum' in summer to minimize self-seeding.
- Sow *Digitalis purpurea* 'Sutton's Apricot' under cover in fall and plant out in spring.
- Cut back main shoots of *Buddleia davidii* by half to three-quarters in the first year. Cut back the previous summer's growth in later years.
- Treat the fennel as a self-seeding biennial and remove old plants as new ones arrive.
- Remove southernwood flowers in late summer.

4 Fill the rest of the bed according to the planting plan. Herbaceous plants are available from fall to spring, and pot-grown varieties are available at any time. Sow from seed or use pot-grown varieties (see "Planting Pot-Grown Herbs," page 96). If you are sowing in open ground, it is advisable to mark the position of the seeds with labels.

2 Goat's rue
(*Galega officinalis* 'Alba')

3 Purple toadflax
(*Linaria purpurea* 'Canon Went')

4 Cardoon
(*Cynara cardunculus*)

3 Apricot foxglove
(*Digitalis purpurea* 'Sutton's Apricot')

2 *Allium aflatunense*

2 Plume poppy
(*Macleaya cordata*)

2 Bloodroot
(*Potentilla erecta*)

2 Turkestan sage
(*Salvia sclaria* 'Turkestanica')

2 Bronze fennel
(*Foeniculum vulgare* 'Purpureum')

4 Bistort
(*Polygonum bistorta*)

2 Bronze fennel
(*Foeniculum vulgare* 'Purpureum')

2 Great mullein
(*Verbascum thapsus*)

4 Golden feverfew
(*Tanacetum parthenium* 'Aureum')

basic techniques

PLANTING POT-GROWN HERBS

1   Carefully remove the herb from the pot and gently loosen the exposed roots.

2   Plant the herb in a hole deep enough to ensure that the surface of the root ball is level with or a little below that of the surrounding soil. (If the herbs are bare-rooted, spread the roots out in the hole.)

3   Crumble the removed soil and firm in around the plant. Try not to compact the soil. Space the herbs appropriately for their final size. Water in well.

MAKING A WOODEN OBELISK

A simple obelisk made from rough-sawn, rot-resistant lumber can be sited in a herb bed or border to add height and structure.

materials and equipment

4 uprights 1½ x 1½ [2 x 2] x 108 in (50 x 50 x 2750 mm)
14 battens 1½ x 1½ [2 x 2] x 48 in (25 x 25 x 1200 mm)
2 boards 1 x 6 x 72 in (25 x 159 x 1800 mm)
nails 1 in (25 mm)

1   Ask your lumber yard to cut each upright on the diagonal to form triangular sections. Arrange the uprights in position on the ground; lay the battens on top of them 7 in (180 mm) apart and nail together. Referring to the diagram below, make sure there is a gap of 1 in (25 mm) between the uprights marked 1 and a gap of 2 in (50 mm) between those marked 2. Cut through the battens to create the sides of the obelisk.

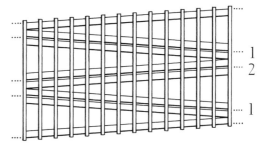

2   Paint or stain the sides, then nail the obelisk together. To create the planter at the bottom of the obelisk, hold the pieces of board against the finished obelisk and mark the angles for cutting. Cut the eight panels to size and nail into place.

DOUBLE DIGGING

All borders should be dug over but they will be better, especially on heavy soils, if they are double dug—as described below—so that the lower layer of earth is also broken up. Do not dig if the soil is too wet. At the same time as the border is dug, as much well-rotted organic matter as possible should be incorporated into the soil.

1 Dig a trench 12–18 in (300–450 mm) wide and 12 in (300 mm) deep. Reserve the removed earth.

2 Work the trench for a further 12 in (300 mm) and add organic matter.

3 Dig out the next trench and use the earth to fill the first one.

4 As before, work through the layer below, breaking up the ground with a fork and adding organic material.

5 When you reach the end of the border, fill the final trench with the reserved earth.

BRACKET TEMPLATE FOR HERB STAGING

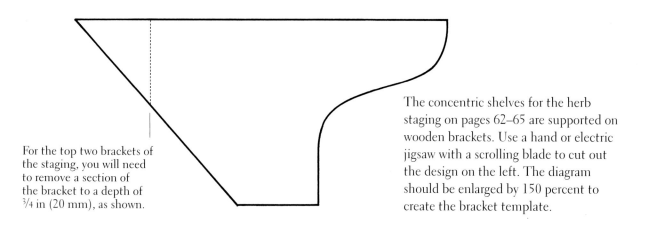

For the top two brackets of the staging, you will need to remove a section of the bracket to a depth of ³/₄ in (20 mm), as shown.

The concentric shelves for the herb staging on pages 62–65 are supported on wooden brackets. Use a hand or electric jigsaw with a scrolling blade to cut out the design on the left. The diagram should be enlarged by 150 percent to create the bracket template.

CUTTING MITERED CORNERS

The most efficient way to cut a mitered joint in a piece of wood is to use a miter box. This simple device has slots to guide the saw. The best type of saw to use for wood that is less than 2 in (50 mm) thick is a tenon saw. Hold the piece of wood against the side of the box and make angled cuts (usually 45°). Square ends can also be cut using the miter box, as shown below.

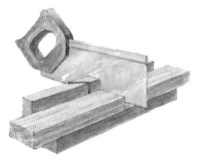

MAKING A TRELLIS PANEL AND CORNER UNIT

Each corner unit of the garden on pages 58–61 consists of two trellis panels mounted onto three corner posts. If it's available, use rough-sawn, pressure-treated lumber, or coat the lumber in exterior-grade wood preservative.

materials & equipment
for each panel
511 in (13 m) lattice* 1 x 2 in (25 x 50 mm)
galvanized finishing nails 1 in (25 mm) long

for each corner unit
3 pressure-treated posts, 3½ x 3½ x 36 [4 x 4]
 (80 x 80 x 900 mm)
3 post anchors
2 pieces lumber ¾ x 2½ x 74 in [1 x 3]
 (25 x 80 x 1830 mm)
timber block for hammering post anchors
sledgehammer
galvanized screws 3 in (80 mm) long
galvanized finishing nails 2 in (50 mm) long

1 From the 1 x 2 (25 x 50 mm) lattice, cut two 74 in (1830 mm) pieces and two 24 in (600 mm) uprights. On the longer pieces mark five equal sections with a pencil. Nail them to the uprights with 1 in (25 mm) nails.

2 From the 1 x 2 (25 x 50 mm) lattice, cut five 31½ in (790 mm) pieces and nail them to the frame at the points marked with a pencil. Cut off the pieces from the diagonals where they overlap the frame, as shown below.

3 From the 1 x 2 (25 x 50 mm) lattice, cut five 31½ in (790 mm) pieces and nail them to the frame in the same way. Cut off the excess wood. Make the second panel.

4 Place the timber block over each of the metal post anchors and hammer them into the ground so the anchor top protrudes only slightly above the soil. Space the anchors at intervals of 74 in (1830 mm).

5 Knock each corner post into a post anchor, as shown.

6 Drill four holes in each of the panel uprights and screw the uprights into the three posts using the galvanized screws.

7 To finish off, nail a 74 in (1830 mm) piece of ¾ x 2½ in (25 x 80 mm) capping to the top of each trellis panel.

*A note about 1 x 2 lattice: Large lumberyards often stock clear pine lattice. If you cannot get this size, ask to have it cut from larger boards.

MAKING A BASIC WINDOW BOX

Follow these instructions to make the basic structures for a raised scented window box (pages 44–47), a balcony herb box (pages 52–55), an herbal window box (pages 66–69).

materials & equipment
screwdriver
power drill with a 1 in (25 mm) spade bit or a brace and bit
wood screws 1½ in (40 mm) long

for a raised scented window box
2 exterior-grade plywood side boards
   ¾ x 6½ x 8 in (20 x 160 x 200 mm)
2 exterior-grade plywood front and back
   boards ¾ x 8 x 36 in (20 x 200 x 900 mm)
2 uprights 1½ x 1½ x 8 in [2 x 2]
   (25 x 25 x 150 mm)
2 battens 1½ x 1½ x 31½ in [2 x 2]
   25 x 25 x 810 mm
2 battens 1½ x 1½ x 3½ in [2 x 2]
   25 x 25 x 110 mm
1 piece of exterior-grade plywood
   ¾ x 6¼ x 34¼ in (20 x 155 x 855 mm)

for each balcony herb box
4 surfaced softwood side boards
   ¾ x 3½ x 8 in [1 x 4] (25 x 100 x 200 mm)
4 surfaced softwood front and back boards
   ¾ x 3½ x 36 in [1 x 4]
   (25 x 100 x 914 mm)
4 uprights 1½ x 1½ x 7 in [2 x 2]
   (25 x 25 x 150 mm)
2 battens 1½ x 1½ x 31½ in [2 x 2]
   (25 x 25 x 800 mm)
2 battens 1½ x 1½ x 5 in [2 x 2]
   (25 x 25 x 150 mm)
1 piece of exterior-grade plywood
   ¾ x 7¾ x 34¼ in (25 x 200 x 850 mm)

for an herbal window box
4 rough-sawn side boards ¾ x 5½ x 10 in
   [1 x 6] (25 x 150 x 250 mm)
4 front and back boards ¾ x 5½ x 31 in
   [1 x 6] (30 x 150 x 780 mm)
4 uprights 1½ x 1½ x 10 in [2 x 2]
   (30 x 30 x 300 mm)
2 battens 1½ x 1½ x 26 in [2 x 2] 25 x 25 x 660 mm
2 battens 1½ x 1½ x 7 in [2 x 2] (25 x 25 x 190 mm)
1 piece of exterior-grade plywood
   ½ x 9¾ x 28¾ in (10 x 245 x 715 mm)

1 Drill pilot holes in each corner of the side boards and screw the side boards to two of the uprights. Attach the remaining side boards to the other two uprights. Note that the raised scented window box is composed of single pieces of plywood.

2 Drill pilot holes in the front and back boards and screw them to the two side boards as shown, ensuring that the bottom boards are flush with the base of the uprights. Turning the box on its side makes this step easier.

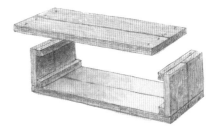

3 Screw the two long battens to the lower boards of the front and back panels from the inside so that they are flush with the base of the box. In the same way, screw the short battens to the lower boards of the side panels.

4 Using a power drill with a 1 in (25 mm) spade bit, drill eight evenly spaced holes in the plywood. Cut a square notch from each corner of the plywood so it fits around the uprights, and slide into position on top of the battens.

care and maintenance

A YEAR IN THE HERB GARDEN

The ideal time to plan the year ahead in your herb garden is at the end of the growing season because—except in years when heavy frosts occur—mid-fall is the best time of year to start planting herbs.

MID-FALL
Container-grown plants can be planted at any time of year but they will become established much better if they are planted in fall or spring. Water the plant thoroughly in its pot before planting. For a dry bare-rooted plant, plunge the root ball into a bucket of water first.
• If you are planting a new herb bed on uncultivated ground, prepare the soil as described in "Double Digging" on page 97.
• Plant trees, shrubs, and hardy herbaceous herbs. Check how far apart they need to be planted based on their ultimate spread, and plant in groups of three, five, or seven, depending on the space available,.
• To prevent invasive herbs such as mint from taking over, plant them in a plastic bucket or other container, which should then be sunk into the ground.
• Move tender herbs in containers into a greenhouse or conservatory.
• Grow parsley and marjoram in pots and overwinter under glass for a winter supply. Cut back larger shrubs.

LATE FALL
• Continue to plant bare-rooted trees and shrubs while the ground is frost-free. Plant low edging such as box, hyssop, rue, and lavender about 9 in (230 mm) apart.
• Cover tender herbs ready for winter.

EARLY WINTER
• Remove soggy herbaceous and annual growth as it dies back, but leave other growth in place to provide winter protection for smaller plants.
• Try to keep the herb garden as neat as you would in the summer.

MIDWINTER
• Now is a good time to think about next year's planting. Order your seeds and plan any alterations or improvements.

LATE WINTER
• Toward the end of the season, sow the seed of tender herbs indoors.
• Plant pot-grown hardy herbaceous herbs and shrubs in frost-free weather.

EARLY SPRING
• Clear away all dead or herbaceous growth. Add a dressing of bonemeal to the ground and fork over the soil.
• Make the first seed sowing of hardy annuals and biennials in the ground if it is not too wet.
• Continue to plant hardy pot-grown herbs in frost-free weather.

MID-SPRING
• Plant container-grown herbs if required.
• Cut back shrubs such as lavender, sage, and santolina to keep them compact.
• Prune larger shrubs to shape.
• Continue to sow seed outdoors and to plant container-grown herbs.
• An annual spring mulch of home-made compost or other organic fertilizer for your herbs would be beneficial.
• Cut back Mediterranean shrubs such as rosemary and lavender to encourge compact new growth.
• Pinch out the growing ends of young shrubs to create a neat shape if required.

LATE SPRING
• Move half hardy and tender plants to a sheltered place so that they can be hardened off for an early summer planting.
• Beware of late frosts.
• Weed from mid-spring to early summer.
• Stake and support any trailing plants.

EARLY SUMMER
• This is perhaps the best season in the herb garden, with the foliage looking fresh and green. Many herbs will now be ready for harvesting.
• Trim dwarf hedges and formal plantings.

MIDSUMMER
• Collect seed from early annuals and biennials for fall or spring sowing and carefully label in separate envelopes.
• Harvest plants for drying and preserving.
• Collect rose petals and lavender flowers for potpourri and sachets.

LATE SUMMER
• Continue to collect petals and scented leaves from plants such as lemon verbena and scented geraniums, and harvest herbs for drying and preserving.
• Collect seed as it ripens.
• Continue to trim formal hedges.

EARLY FALL
• Dig up tender and half-hardy plants and overwinter in pots under glass or inside.
• Fork over the soil and fertilize any permanent planting.

HARVESTING AND DRYING
Harvest herbs on a dry, sunny morning after any moisture has evaporated from the leaves but before they are exposed to full sun. Handle aromatic herbs as little as possible to avoid bruising them and releasing the volatile oils. Foliage is usually harvested just before the flowers appear.

Small-leaved herbs should be dried in small bunches on the stem. Leaves should then be removed from the stem and stored in sealed containers. Dry whole flowers off the stalk face up on a tray lined with paper.

HERBS IN CONTAINERS
There are a number of advantages to growing herbs in containers. For example, it allows you to position culinary herbs conveniently near the kitchen door so that you can harvest your herbs as and when required. Growing tender herbs such as basil in containers means that they can easily be moved under glass or into a conservatory to overwinter.

You can also control the soil and growing conditions in a container far more easily than you can in a garden. Depending on the requirements of a particular herb, you can provide, for example, sharp-draining sandy soil or moist peaty soil. Many herbs enjoy the free-draining dryish conditions that can be created by container culture.

PLANTING CONTAINERS
When planting your containers, make sure the soil you use is suited to the type of herb. In a mixed planting, it is important to consider how large the herbs will eventually become and whether some may overwhelm others, although this can be corrected with pruning and annual division.

Check the moisture level of the soil in the containers on a daily basis and water every day. Water thoroughly from late spring throughout the growing season.

The best time to water pot-grown herbs is in the early morning or evening. Make sure there is at least 1 in (25 mm) between the top of the soil and the pot in order to provide a watering reservoir. Feed the herb with a liquid fertilizer at least once every two weeks during the growing season.

If your herbs become pot-bound—with their roots protruding from the base of the container—repot in spring. Either replant in a larger pot or simply divide the plant and repot into two or more pots.

herb directory

key   H = height   S = spread   Z = zones

Zone classifications are based on the average annual minimum temperature for each zone; the smaller number indicates the most northerly zone a plant can survive in; the higher number the most southerly zone the plant will tolerate.

Z1: below -50°F (-45°C)
Z2: -50 to -40°F (-45 to -40°C)
Z3: -40 to -30°F (-40 to -34°C)
Z4: -30 to -20°F (-34 to - 29°C)
Z5: -20 to -10°F (-29 to 23°C)
Z6: -10 to 0°F (-23 to - 18°C)
Z7: 0 to 10°F (-18 to -12°C)
Z8: 10 to 20°F (-12 to -7°C)
Z9: 20 to 30°F (-7 to -1°C)
Z10: 30 to 40°F (-1 to 4°C)
Z11: above 40°F (4°C)

Achillea millefolium (Yarrow, milfoil)
H: 2–12 in (5–30 cm); S: 2–8 in (5–20 cm); Z: 3–9
A perennial with white to pink flower heads.
It prefers a well-drained soil in full sun.

Agrimonia eupatoria (Agrimony, sticklewort)
H: 1–2 ft (30–60 cm);
S: 8–12 in (20–30 cm); Z: 6–9
A hardy perennial with yellow flowers in summer. It will tolerate alkaline soil but prefers soil to be well drained.

Ajuga reptans (Bugle)
H: 4–12 in (10–30 cm); S: indefinite; Z: 3–9
An evergreen perennial with blue flowers and varied leaf color. Prefers moist soil but grows well either in sun or shade. Other bugles include bronze bugle (A. *reptans* 'Atropurpurea'), which has purplish, dark brown foliage, and A. *reptans* 'Burgundy Glow,' which has bronze and pink foliage and grows to only 3–6 in (8–15 cm).

Alchemilla mollis (Lady's mantle)
H and S: 20 in (50 cm); Z :4–7
A perennial with striking bright green foliage and yellow-green flowers in late spring to summer. Prefers moist well-drained soil in sun or partial shade.

Allium (Onion)
Alliums prefer a well-drained soil and full sun or partial shade, although chives will tolerate a damper soil and more shade.
A. aflatunense
H: 2–3 ft (60–90 cm); S: 1 ft (30 cm); Z: 4–8
A decorative member of the onion family with large dense heads of purple flowers in early summer.
A. cristophii
H: 2 ft (60 cm); Z: 4–8
Silver-lilac flower heads made of many large star-shaped flowers.
A. schoenoprasum (Chives)
H: 4–24 in (10–60 cm); S: 12 in (30 cm); Z: 3–9
A clump-forming allium with thin hollow leaves and purple to pink flowers in summer. Cut back after flowering.
A. tuberosum (Chinese chives, garlic chives)
H and S: 20 in (47 cm); Z: 3–9
A perennial with flat leaves and scented star-shaped flowers in later summer.

Anethum graveolens (Dill)
H: 2–3 ft (60–90 cm); S: 6–12 in (15–30 cm)
An annual or biennial with a hollow stem and thread-like foliage. The yellow summer flowers produce fragrant seeds. Prefers well-drained neutral soil in sun.

Angelica archangelica (Angelica)
H: 3–8 ft (90–250 cm); S: 1½–3½ ft (45–100 cm); Z: 4–9
A biennial or perennial with umbels of small green-white flowers in early summer, followed by beautiful seed-heads. This grandly architectural plant self-seeds readily and prefers moist soil in sun or partial shade.

Anthriscus cerefolium (Chervil)
H: 1–2 ft (30–60 cm); S: 9–12 in (23–30 cm); Z: 3–8
A biennial with bright green divided leaves and white flowers in early summer. It is a bitter aniseed-flavored culinary herb that prefers damp soil in partial shade.

Artemisia (Wormwood, sage brush)
A genus of hardy and half-hardy subshrubs, annuals, biennials, and perennials, grown for their finely cut foliage. They need sun and well-drained, preferably alkaline soil. Cut back hard in spring.

A. abrotanum (Southernwood)
H: 3 ft (90 cm); S: 1–2 ft (30–60 cm); Z: 6–10
A semi-evergreen grayish green subshrub with yellow flowers in hot summers.

A. absinthium (Wormwood)
H: 3 ft (90 cm); S: 2–3 ft (60–90 cm); Z: 6–10
A silver-gray sub-shrub with feathery leaves and small yellow flowers in summer.

A. dracunculus (French tarragon)
H: 1½–3 ft (45–100 cm); S: 12–15 in (30–38 cm); Z: 4–7
An aromatic perennial culinary herb with long thin leaves and small green flowers that will fail to open in cool summers. Leaves used with chicken, eggs, and salad dressings. Protect from frost.

A. 'Powis Castle'
H: 2–3 ft (60–90 cm); S: 4 ft (1.2 m); Z: 6–9
A dwarf variety with silver leaves and no flowers.

Borago officinalis (Borage)
H: 1–3 ft (30–90 cm); S: 6–12 in (15–30 cm)
An annual with bright green fleshy leaves and five-petalled blue flowers. Prefers well-drained moist soil and sun.

Buxus sempervirens (Common boxwood)
H: 6–15 ft (2–5 m);
S: 4–6 ft (1.2–2 m); Z: 5–8
A dark green evergreen shrub ideal for edging and topiary. Silver boxwood (*B. sempervirens* 'Elegantissima') has white-edged pale green leaves. It is dwarf and slow growing. Edging boxwood (*B. sempervirens* 'Suffruticosa') has a height and spread of 2½ ft (75 cm); its leaves are more oval and a slightly brighter green. It is slow growing and compact. Boxwood prefers well-drained soil and sun or shade. Cut back hard to encourage new growth in spring and clip in late summer.

Centaurea (Knapweed)
A group of thistle-like meadow flowers that appear in summer and will attract bees and butterflies. They prefer full sun and well-drained alkaline soil.

C. nigra (Common knapweed)
H and S: 1–2 ft (30–60 cm); Z: 3–7
A perennial with reddish purple flowers from early summer to early fall. Found in meadows and hedgerows.

C. scabiosa (Greater knapweed)
H and S: 1–2 ft (30–60 cm); Z: 3–7
An attractive plant with divided leaves and large pink flower heads.

Chamaemelum nobile (Chamomile)
H: 6 in (15 cm); S: 18 in (45 cm); Z: 4–8
An evergreen perennial that forms an aromatic green mat with yellow-and-white daisy-like flowers. Prefers well-drained soil in sun. *C. nobile* 'Flore Pleno' has double flowers. Non-flowering lawn chamomile (*C. nobile* 'Treneague') grows to a height of only 1 in (2.5 cm).

Cynara cardunculus (Cardoon)
H: 6 ft (2 m); S: 3 ft (90 cm); Z: 9
A giant perennial with gray architectural leaves. The blue thistle-like flowers appear in summer. It needs full sun and may need protection during winter in cooler areas.

Dianthus caryophyllus (Clove pink)
H: 8–20 in (20–50 cm);
S: 4–10 in (10–25 cm); Z: 5–8
An evergreen perennial with grayish green foliage and small pink to purple scented flowers in summer. Use the flower heads in pot-pourris and salads. Prefers well-drained neutral to alkaline soil and sun.

Digitalis purpurea (Foxglove)
H: 3 ft (90 cm); S: 10 in (25 cm); Z: 4–9
Self-seeding biennial with rough mid- to dark green leaves and tall spires in shades of pink and white. Prefers dry conditions and partial shade. All species are poisonous.

Eryngium
A genus of biennials and perennials with architectural, usually silvery green foliage. They prefer full sun and well-drained soils.

E. agavifolium (Sea holly)
H: 4–5 ft (1.2–1.5 m); S: 1½–2 ft (45–60 cm); Z: 6–9
A good architectural perennial with pointed agave-like leaves and thistle-like green-white flowers in summer.

E. x tripartitum
H: 3 ft (90 cm); S: 1½–2 ft (45–60 cm); Z: 4–8
A perennial with coarsely toothed leaves and striking blue-gray teasel-like flowers in summer. Prefers full sun and dry soils.

Foeniculum vulgare (Fennel)
H: 6 ft (1.8 m); S: 1½ ft (45 cm); Z: 4–10
A hardy biennial or perennial with hollow stems, feathery soft green leaves and yellow flat-headed flowers in summer. Prefers well-drained soil in full sun. *F. vulgare* 'Purpureum' has striking deep bronze foliage, it self-seeds and grows to a height of 4–5 ft (1.2–1.5 m), while sweet fennel (*F. vulgare dulce*) grows to only 2 ft (60 cm). The stalk bases of this fennel develop to form a white bulbous aniseed-flavored vegetable.

Fragaria vesca (Wild strawberry)
H: 10 in (25 cm); S: 8 in (20 cm); Z: 5–9
A hardy perennial that spreads by long runners, with green serrated leaves. Flowers with four or five white petals and yellow centers appear in spring to early summer and are followed by small red fruits. It requires rich soil in sun or partial shade. The name "strawberry" is derived from the Anglo-Saxon word "straw," meaning small particles of chaff, which refers to the scattering of pips (achenes) on the surface of the fruit.

Galega officinalis 'Alba' (Goat's rue)
H: 3–5 ft (90–150 cm);
S: 2–3 ft (60–90 cm); Z: 3–9
A perennial with spikes of white
pea-like flowers in summer. Prefers
well-drained soil and sun or partial shade.

Galium odoratum (Woodruff)
H: 20 in (50 cm); S: indefinite; Z: 3–9
A creeping perennial with white star-shaped
flowers in early summer and bright green
leaves. Prefers moist well-drained soil in shade.

Helichrysum italicum (Curry plant)
H: 2 ft (60 cm); S: 3 ft (90 cm); Z: 8–9
An evergreen sub-shrub with fine silver
leaves and yellow flowers in summer.
It smells of curry after rain. Prefers
well-drained soil in sun.

Hyssopus officinalis (Hyssop)
H: 1½–2 ft (45–60 cm);
S: 2–3 ft (60–90 cm); Z: 3–9
A semi-evergreen perennial with
purple-blue flower spikes in summer.
H. officinalis roseus has bright pink
flowers, while *H. officinalis albus* is ideal
for white gardens. The more compact
rock hyssop (*H. officinalis aristatus*) has
a height and spread of only 1 ft (30 cm).
Prefers well-drained to dry soil. Cut back
hard in spring in order to keep a compact shape.

Laurus nobilis (Sweet bay, bay laurel)
H: 10–50 ft (3–15 m); S: 30 ft (9 m); Z: 8–10
A dense evergreen shrub with beautiful bright
green foliage and leathery, aromatic, pointed
leaves. Small cream flowers appear in the spring.
It is ideal for training into a standard or pyramid.
Trim and pinch out the ends of the shoots in
summer when training the standard to encourage
a compact head.

Lavandula (Lavender)
A genus of aromatic, evergreen, mainly summer-
flowering perennials and shrubs. Lavenders differ
in habit, foliage, and flower color and many make
effective low hedges. They prefer chalky, well-drained
soils and a sheltered site that gets plenty of sun.
L. angustifolia (English lavender)
H and S: 9 in–3 ft (23–90 cm); Z: 5–8
A small shrub with downy leaves, which are white at
first and then become greener, and tiny purple flowers
in the summer. There are a variety of cultivars of different
heights and spreads. 'Hidcote' is a very popular cultivar
for hedging, with an erect habit, gray leaves, and strongly
scented deep violet flowers in early summer. 'Munstead'
is an early-flowering cultivar with small leaves and bright
lavender-blue flowers. 'Rosea' is the original pink lavender
with green rather than gray-green leaves.

L. x intermedia (Lavandin)
H and S: 2–3 ft (60–90 cm); Z: 5–7
A species with grayish green leaves and highly
scented white flowers from mid to late summer.
L. 'Sawyers'
H: 1½–2 ft (45–60 cm); S: 3 ft (90 cm); Z: 7–9
A hybrid lavender with gray leaves and lavender-blue
flowers that open to purple.
L. stoechas (French lavender, Spanish lavender)
H and S: 1–3 ft (30–90 cm); Z: 8–9
A shrub with light green leaves and purple flowers
with purple bracts. In a sheltered position this
type of lavender will be hardy in cold areas.

Levisticum officinale (Lovage)
H: 6 ft (1.8 m); S: 3 ft (90 cm); Z: 5–8
A large perennial with small yellow flowers
in summer followed by aromatic seeds.
Prefers rich moist soil in sun or shade.

Linaria (Toadflax)
A genus of annuals and perennials that
prefer well-drained soil and either sun
or partial shade.
L. purpurea 'Canon Went' (Purple toadflax)
H: 2–3 ft (60–90 cm);
S: 1–1½ ft (30–45 cm); Z: 6–9
A perennial with orange-pink summer
flowers that prefers sun and a light soil.
L. vulgaris (Common toadflax)
H: 6–36 in (15–90 cm);
S: 4–18 in (10–45 cm); Z: 6–9
An upright perennial with yellow flowers
from summer to fall. Prefers well-drained
soil in sun or partial shade.

Linum perenne (Flax)
H: 1–1½ ft (30–45 cm); S: 1 ft (30 cm); Z: 4–9
A perennial with sky-blue flowers from early
summer to early fall.

Malva moschata (Musk mallow)
H : 1–2 ft (30–60 cm); S: 2 ft (60 cm);
Z: 3–5
Mallows make attractive border plants
and are easily grown in poor soils.
This species has delicate pink flowers.
Prefers well-drained poor soil in sun
or partial shade.

Melissa officinalis (Lemon balm)
H: 12–32 in (30–80 cm); S: 12–18 in
(30–45 cm); Z: 4–9
A perennial with lemon-scented toothed
green leaves and yellow flowers in
summer. Prefers moist soil in sun or
partial shade. Gold lemon balm (*M. officinalis*
'Aurea'), with yellow variegated leaves, and
sun-loving *M. officinalis* 'All Gold,' which has
bright gold foliage, grow to only 30–60 cm (1–2 ft).

Mentha (Mint)
All the mints listed here are perennial and prefer
a rich moist soil in sun or partial shade. Mints
are invasive and should be grown in buckets
sunk into the ground.
M. x **gracilis** (Gingermint, redmint)
H: 1–3 ft (30–90 cm); S: indefinite; Z: 7–9
A sweetly scented mint with lilac flowers in summer.
M. x gracilis 'Variegata' has yellow variegated
fruit-scented leaves.
M. x **longifolia** (Horsemint)
H: 16–48 in (40–120 cm); S: indefinite; Z: 6–9
A downy grayish mint with peppermint-scented
leaves and lilac or white flowers.
M. x **piperita** (Peppermint)
H: 1–3 ft (30–90 cm); S: indefinite; Z: 4–9
This creeping variety has purple-tinged leaves.
Eau de cologne mint (M. x piperata 'Citrata')
has bronze-purple leaves and a lavender scent.
M. pulegium (Pennyroyal)
H: 4–16 in (10–40 cm); S: indefinite; Z: 6–9
A low creeping perennial with small ovate leaves.
M. x **smithiana** (Red raripila mint)
H: 20 in–5 ft (50cm–1.5 m); S: indefinite; Z: 7–9
A creeping perennial with purple flowers.
M. spicata (Common mint, spearmint)
H: 1–3 ft (30–90 cm); S: indefinite; Z: 4–9
A perennial mint with purple-tinged leaves
and lilac-pink or white flowers.
M. suaveolens 'Variegata' (Pineapple mint)
H: 16–36 in (40–90 cm); S: indefinite; Z: 7–9
This lovely mint has creamy white variegated
leaves with a fruity fragrance.

Monarda fistulosa (Wild bergamot)
H: 4 ft (1.2 m); S: 1¹/₂ ft (45 cm); Z: 3–9
A perennial with gray-green leaves and lilac
to pink flowers in summer to fall. Prefers
rich moist soil and full sun.

Myrtus communis (Myrtle)
H and S: 10 ft (3 m); Z: 9–10
An evergreen shrub that can make a dense
hedge in mild areas. Its aromatic ovate-
lanceolate leaves are dark green and glossy.
From spring to midsummer it has fragrant
white flowers with clusters of gold stamen,
followed by purple-black fruits. Prefers
well-drained neutral to alkaline soil in
full sun. Trim in spring and remove
damaged or dead shoots.

Nepeta (Catnip, catmint)
A genus of popular perennials for the
herb garden which should be cut back
hard after flowering to encourage a
second flush. Prefers moist well-drained
soil in sun. Its common name derives
from its stimulant effect on cats, which
eat and roll in the plant.

N. cataria (Catnip, catmint)
H: 1–3 ft (30–90 cm); S: 9–24 in (23–60 cm); Z: 4–9
A pungent perennial with erect branched
stems and gray-green ovate toothed leaves.
The white, purple-spotted, tubular flowers
appear from summer to mid-fall.
N. x **faassenii** (Catmint)
H and S: 1¹/₂ ft (45 cm); Z: 4–9
A hardy perennial that forms bushy clumps with
small grayish green aromatic leaves and spikes of
lavender-blue flowers in early summer. This hybrid
is popular on account of its ornamental appeal.
N. 'Six Hills Giant'
H: 2 ft (60 cm); S: 3 ft (90 cm); Z: 4–9
A fast-growing perennial with mauve-blue flowers
in summer.

Ocimum basilicum (Basil, sweet basil)
H: 8–24 in (20–60 cm); S: 6–18 in (15–45 cm)
An annual culinary herb with aromatic green
leaves and white tubular flowers. O. basilicum
'Anise' has purplish foliage, pink flower spikes,
and an aniseed-like aroma. O. basilicum
purpurascens has purple foliage, and the
dwarf Greek basil (O. basilicum minimum)
has white flowers. Prefers rich well-drained
to dry soil in sun.

Origanum (Marjoram)
A group of perennials and sub-shrubs that prefer
well-drained to dry, neutral to alkaline soil in sun.
O. marjorana (Sweet marjoram)
H: 2 ft (60 cm); S: 1¹/₂ ft (45 cm); Z: 9–10
It has red-brown stems, downy gray-green leaves
and white to pink flowers from late summer.
O. onites (Pot marjoram, Greek oregano)
H and S: 24 in (60 cm)
A perennial with downy leaves and white, often
purplish flowers in summer and early fall.
O. vulgare (Wild marjoram, oregano)
H and S: 1¹/₂–2¹/₂ ft (45–75 cm); Z: 7–9
A bushy species with purple-brown stems,
ovate leaves and clusters of pink flowers in
summer. 'Gold Tip' has yellow variegated foliage
in spring. 'Country Cream' has variegated
foliage, and golden marjoram (O. vulgare
'Aureum') has yellow-green leaves.

Petroselinum crispum (Parsley)
H: 12–32 in (30–80 cm);
S: 12 in (30 cm); Z: 6–9
An aromatic biennial with triangular leaves
and tiny yellow-green flowers in summer. It
prefers rich well-drained neutral to alkaline
soil in sun or partial shade. P. crispum 'Moss
Curled' grows to only 1 ft (30 cm) tall but has
densely curled foliage. The hardier French
parsley (P. crispum 'Italian') has a height and
spread of 15–24 in (38–60 cm) and flat dark
green foliage.

Polygonum bistorta (bistort, snakeweed)
H: 1¹/₂ ft (45 cm); S: 1 ft (30 cm); Z: 3–9
A clump-forming perennial with handsome, broadly ovate leaves. Pink flowers appear in dense spikes in summer, followed by hard nutlets.

Potentilla erecta (Bloodroot)
H: 20 in (50 cm); S: 12 in (30 cm); Z: 3–9
A perennial with a woody root stock and branched stems. Small yellow four-petalled flowers appear from early summer. Prefers sun or light shade.

Rosmarinus officinalis (Rosemary)
H: 6 ft (1.8 m);
S: 5–6 ft (1.5–1.8 m); Z: 8–10
An aromatic evergreen shrub with blunt-ended needle-like leaves and tubular two-lipped flowers in spring. The flowers are pale to dark blue, rarely pink or white. It prefers well-drained neutral to alkaline soil in sun but will need shelter in cold areas. Prune after flowering and remove old stems and straggly shoots in spring.

Ruta graveolens (Rue)
H: 2 ft (60 cm);
S: 1¹/₂ ft (45 cm); Z: 4–8
A group of evergreen or semi-evergreen subshrubs that prefer well-drained neutral to alkaline soil in sun. 'Jackman's Blue' has blue-gray leaves, while variegated rue (R. graveolens 'Variegata') has creamy white markings and the occasional white leaf.

Salvia (Sage)
A group of culinary herbs that prefer well-drained to dry, neutral to alkaline soil in sun. Replace when the plants become sparse or woody.
S. elegans (Tangerine sage)
H and S: 3 ft (90 cm); Z: 9–10
An evergreen perennial with green pineapple-scented leaves. Spikes of red to pink flowers appear in winter.
S. officinalis (Common sage)
H: 24–32 in (60–80 cm);
S: 3 ft (1m); Z: 5–8
A shrubby evergreen perennial with velvety gray-green leaves and spikes of violet to purple, pink or white flowers in summer. Purple sage (S. officinalis Purpurascens Group) has purple-gray foliage, while S. officinalis 'Icterina' has yellow variegated leaves. 'Kew Gold' grows to a height of only 12 in (30 cm).

S. sclarea turkestanica
H: 3 ft (90 cm); S: 2 ft (60 cm); Z: 4–9
A colorful variety with pink stems, pink to white bracts and pale blue and white flowers.

Santolina chamaecyparissus (Cotton lavender)
H: 8–20 in (20–50 cm); S: 24 in (60 cm); Z: 6–8
An aromatic shrub with white leaves and yellow flowers in summer. Prefers light well-drained to dry soil in sun, but tolerates sandy or poor alkaline soils. Trim in fall and cut back hard in spring.

Saponaria officinalis (Soapwort)
H: 1–3 ft (30–90 cm); S: 2 ft (60 cm); Z: 2–8
A rhizomatous perennial with pointed leaves and scented pale pink flowers from midsummer to mid-fall. It prefers moist well-drained neutral to alkaline soil in sun or partial shade.

Satureja (Savory)
A group of ornamental herbs that prefer well-drained to dry, neutral to alkaline soil in sun. Pinch out new shoots in spring and cut back in fall or spring.
S. hortensis (Summer savory)
H: 4–15 in (10–38 cm); S: 7–30 in (17–75 cm)
An annual with a single widely branched stem and short stalked leaves. The lilac to white or purple flowers appear in summer.
S. montana (Winter savory)
H: 4–16 in (10–40 cm); S: 3–8 in (8–20 cm)
A shrubby evergreen culinary perennial with pointed leaves and whorls of white to pale pink or purple flowers in summer.

Symphytum (Comfrey)
A group of ornamental herbs that prefer moist to wet soil in sun or partial shade.
S. officinale (Comfrey, knitbone)
H: 2–4 ft (60–120 cm); S: 1–2 ft (30–60 cm); Z: 4–9
A bristly haired perennial with large ovate to lanceolate leaves and purple to white funnel-shaped flowers in summer.
S. x uplandicum (Russian comfrey)
H: 6 ft (1.8 m); S: 3 ft (90 cm); Z: 4–8
A comfrey with pink flowers that turn blue as they age. S. x uplandicum 'Variegatum', which grows to only 3 ft (90 cm), has irregular ivory variegation.

Tanacetum (Tansy)
This group of hardy annuals and perennials prefer well-drained to dry stony soil in sun. Remove flower heads to prevent excessive self-seeding.
T. densum
H: 6 in (15 cm); S: indefinite; Z: 7–9
A species with feathery gray leaves that make a good gray ground cover.
T. parthenium 'Aureum' (Golden feverfew)
H and S: 8–18 in (20–45 cm); Z: 4–9
A particularly outstanding cultivar with striking golden foliage.

T. vulgare (Tansy)
H: 2–4 ft (60–120 cm); S: indefinite;
Z: 4–9
A strongly aromatic perennial with dark
green leaves and clusters of yellow button-
like flowers in late summer and fall.
T. vulgare crispum grows to only 2 ft (60
cm) and has finely cut leaves in spring.

Teucrium (Germander)
A group of perennials and shrubs that
prefer well-drained to dry soil in sun.
T. chamaedrys (Wall germander)
H and S: 4–10 in (10–25 cm); Z: 5–9
A shrubby perennial useful for low hedges
with upright to spreading stems and shiny
aromatic leaves. Small purple-pink tubular
flowers appear in summer and fall. Cut off dead
flower spikes to encourage bushy new growth.
T. fruticans (Tree germander)
H: 1 ft (30 cm); S: 3 ft (90 cm); Z: 8–10
A perennial, with gray foliage and pale
blue-lilac flowers in summer.

Thymus (Thyme)
A group of hardy herbs that prefer well-
drained soil in sun. They grow well in
gravel and in the cracks of paving. Trim
after flowering to encourage growth.
T. x citriodorus (Lemon thyme)
H: 10–12 in (25–30 cm);
S: 60 cm (24 in); Z: 5–9
A species with lemon-scented leaves
and pale lilac flowers. *T. x citriodorus*
'Bertram Anderson' grows to only
6–9 in (15–23 cm) and has golden foliage.
Golden lemon thyme (*T. x citriodorus*
'Aureus') has gold-splashed leaves with
a height of 4–6 in (10–15 cm). 'Archer's Gold'
grows to only 6–9 in (15–23 cm) and has bright yellow
compact foliage and pale purple flowers. The leaves
of 'Silver Queen' are tinged with pink in winter.
T. 'Doone Valley'
H: 4–6 in (10–15 cm); S: 18 in (45 cm)
A cultivar with purple flowers and green-and-gold leaves
with a lemon scent.
T. herba-barona (Caraway thyme)
H: 2–4 in (5–10 cm); S: 24 in (60 cm); Z: 6–8
A spreading sub-shrub with tiny, dark green leaves,
which smell of caraway, and pink to mauve flowers
in midsummer.
T. polytrichus (Creeping thyme)
H: 2 in (5 cm); S: 18 in (45 cm); Z: 5–8
A mat-forming thyme with hair-fringed leaves and purple
flowers in summer.
T. 'Porlock'
H: 4–6 in (10–15 cm);
S: 18 in (45 cm); Z: 5–8
A cultivar with purple flowers and green-and-gold leaves
with a lemon scent.

T. pseudolanuginosus (Woolly thyme)
H: 1–3 in (2–9 cm); S: 3 ft (90 cm); Z: 6–8
A very recognizable shrublet forming a dense
mat of gray-green woolly leaves with a few pale
pink flowers in midsummer.
T. serpyllum (Wild thyme)
H: 1–3 in (2–9 cm); S: 3 ft (90 cm); Z: 4–8
A perennial with pink flowers in summer.
'Annie Hall' has pale green leaves and pink
flowers. 'Pink Chintz' has grayish green leaves
and a spread of only 60 cm (2 ft). 'Lemon Curd'
has lemon-scented leaves and pink flowers,
while 'Russetings' has bronze-tinted foliage
with a height of 1–7 cm (½–3 in). Red-flowered
thyme (*T. serpyllum coccineus*) has crimson-pink flowers.
T. vulgaris (Common thyme)
H: 1–1½ ft (30–45 cm); S: 2 ft (60 cm); Z: 4–8
An upright shrub with grayish green leaves and white
to pale purple flowers. Silver thyme (*T. vulgaris* 'Silver
Posie') grows to only 10 in (25 cm) and has gray
variegated leaves and pale mauve flowers. *T. vulgaris
aureus* is an attractive golden thyme. *T. vulgaris albus*
is a low-growing thyme with white flowers.

Tropaeolum majus (Nasturtium)
H: 10 ft (3 m); S: 5–6 ft (1.5–1.8 m)
A fast-growing trailing annual with almost circular
leaves and yellow to orange scented flowers. Prefers
moist well-drained average to poor soil in sun.

Valeriana officinalis
H: 5 ft (1.5 m); S: 4 ft (1.2 m); Z: 5–9
A perennial with irregularly divided leaves
and dense clusters of small pink or white
flowers in summer, followed by tiny seeds
with a tuft of white hairs. Valerian prefers
moist soil in sun or shade.

Verbascum thapsus (Great mullein)
H: 6 ft (1.8 m): S: 3 ft (90 cm); Z: 5–9
A tall biennial with soft gray-green woolly
leaves that form a basal rosette in the
first year. The yellow flowers are borne
in a dense terminal spike in summer.
Mullein prefers well-drained to dry
soil in sun.

Verbena officinalis (Vervain)
H: 32 in (80 cm);
S: 24 in (60 cm); Z: 4–8
A perennial with pinnate leaves and tiny
lilac flowers on slender spikes in summer.
Prefers well-drained moist soil in sun.

Viola tricolor (Heartsease, wild pansy)
H and S: 15 in (38 cm); Z: 4–9
A small pansy flower in various combinations
of purple, lilac, white, and yellow in spring and
summer. Prefers well-drained but moist soil in
sun or partial shade.

resources

PLANT SUPPLIERS AND NURSERIES

Avant Gardens
710 High Hill Road
North Dartmouth
MA 02747-1363
(508) 998-8819
www.avantgardensNE.com

Bluestone Perennials
7211 Middle Ridge Road
Madison, OH 44057-3096
(800) 852-5243
www.bluestoneperennials.com

W. Atlee Burpee Seed Co.
300 Park Avenue
Warminster, PA 18974
(800) 888-1447
www.burpee.com

Carroll Gardens
444 E. Main Street
Westminster, MD 21157
(800) 638-6334
www.carrollgardens.com

Catnip Acres Herb Farm
67 Christian Street
Oxford, CT 06478
(203) 888-5649
www.catnipacres.com

Companion Plants
7247 N. Collville Ridge Road
Athens, OH 45701
(740) 592-4643
www.companionplants.com

The Cook's Garden
P.O. Box 535
Londonderry, VT 05148
(800) 547-9703
www. cooksgarden.com

DeBaggio Herbs
Catalog Dept.
43494 Mountain View Drive
Chantilly, VA 20152
(703) 327-6976
www.debaggioherbs.com

Filaree Farm
182 Conconully Hwy
Okanogan, WA 98840
(509) 422 6940
www.filareefarm.com

Goodwin Creek Gardens
P.O. Box 83
Williams, OR 97544
(800) 846-7359
www.goodwincreekgardens.com

Heronswood Nursery
7530 NE 288th Street
Kingston, WA 98346
(360) 297-4172
www.heronswood.com

Logee's Greenhouses
141 North Street
Danielson, CT 06239
(888) 330-8038
www.logees.com

Mellinger's Inc.
2310 W. South Range Road
North Lima, OH 44452
(800) 321-7444
www.mellingers.com

Nichols Garden Nursery
1190 Old Salem Road NE
Albany, OR 97321
(541) 928-9280
www.nicholsgardennursery.com

Peaceful Valley Farm Supply
P.O. Box 2209
Grass Valley, CA 95945
(888) 784-1722
www.groworganic.com

Piedmont Plant Company
807 N. Washington Street
P.O. Box 424
Albany, GA 31702
(800) 541-5185
www.plantfields.com

Sandy Mush Herb Nursery
316 Surrett Cove Rd
Leicester, NC 28748
(828) 683-2014

The Thyme Garden
20546 Alsea Highway
Alsea, OR 97324
(541) 487-8671
www.thymegarden.com

Tinmouth Channel Farm
P.O. Box 428 B
Tinmouth, VT 05773
(802) 446-2812

Wayside Gardens
1 Garden Lane
Hodges, SC 29695-0001
(800) 845-1124
www.waysidegardens.com

White Flower Farm
P.O. Box 50
Litchfield, CT 06759
(800) 503-9624
www.whiteflowerfarm.com

MATERIALS AND TOOLS

Ace Hardware Corporation
2200 Kensington Ct.
Oak Brook, IL 60523-2100
(630) 990-6600
www.acehardware.com
Hardware from A to Z with seasonal gardening supplies.

Lowe's Home Centers
Located throughout
the U.S.A.
(800) 445-6937
www.lowes.com
A nationwide chain warehouse of home improvement supplies.

The Home Depot
2455 Paces Ferry Road
Atlanta, GA 30339
(800) 430-3376
www.homedepot.com
Chain store with home and garden supplies and materials.

Sears, Roebuck
(800) MY-SEARS
www.sears.com
*Garden products available
through catalog, retail outlets,
and online store.*

GARDEN SUPPLIES

Dan's Garden Shop
5821 Woodwinds Circle
Frederick, MD 21703
(301) 662-3572
www.dansgardenshop.com

Gardener's Supply Company
128 Intervale Rd.
Burlington, VT 05401
(888) 833-1412
www.gardeners.com
*Tools, containers, soil, seed,
and everything for the garden.*

**Home Harvest Garden
Supply Inc.**
3807 Bank Street
Baltimore, MD 21224
(800) 348-4769
www.homeharvest.com
*Wide variety and selection,
with lots of pots.*

Kinsman Company
River Road
Point Pleasant
PA 18950-0357
(800) 733-4146
www.kinsmangarden.com
*Classy garden items, including
moss-lined baskets and troughs.*

Kmart
(800) 355-6388
www.kmart.com
Chain store with locations
throughout the U.S.A.
*Gardening supplies and
seasonal flowers.*

Simple Gardens
615 Old Cemetery Road
Richmond, VT 05477
(800) 351-2438
www.simplegarden.com
*General gardening supplies,
especially for small gardens.*

Smith and Hawken
Two Arbor Lane
Box 6900
Florence, KY 41022-6900
(800) 981-9888
www.smith-hawken.com
*Mail-order garden supplies,
ornaments, and specialties.*

Target Stores
33 South Sixth Street
Minneapolis, MN 55402
(888) 304-4000
www.target.com
*Modern variety store with
craft needs and accessories
for outdoor living.*

Walt Nicke's Garden Talk
P.O. Box 433
Topsfield, MA 01983
(978) 887-3388
www.gardentalk.com
*Fine tools and garden
ornaments.*

CONTAINERS

Brooks Barrel Company
5228 Bucktown Rd.
P.O. Box 1056
Cambridge, MD 21613
(800) 398-2766
*Handcrafted wooden barrels,
kegs and planters of all sizes.*

Karen Harris
200 East Genesee St.
Fayetteville, NY 13066
*Handmade hypertufa
garden troughs.*

Master Garden Products
15650 SE 9th St.
Bellevue, WA 98008
(425) 401-1083
www.mastergardenproducts.com
Teak tubs and barrels.

Martha by Mail
P.O. Box 60060
Tampa, FL 33660-0060
(800) 950-7130
www.marthabymail.com
Unusual containers and urns.

Windowbox.com
817 San Julian St., Suite 406
Los Angeles, CA 90014
(888) GARDEN-Box
www.windowbox.com
*Especially for the rooftop or
balcony gardener; online advice.*

credits

The projects in this book were designed by George Carter except for the following:
A thyme bed (pages 18–21): designer Lower Severalls, Somerset. A small knot garden (pages 26–29): designer The Lady Tollemache, Helmingham Hall. A scented bed (pages 36–39): designers Brian and Rosemary Clifton-Sprigg, Norfolk Herbs. A small brick-edged herb garden (pages 70–73): designer Anthony O'Grady, head gardener, Penshurst Place, Kent. An informal herb bed (pages 80–83): designer Patricia Hardcastle. A flowery mead (pages 84–87): designer Countryside Wildflowers, Marnie Hall. A herb-lined pathway (pages 88–91):

designer Lucy Huntington. Herbs with architectural foliage (pages 92–95): designer Ethne Clarke.

The photographs were taken by Marianne Majerus except those for the endpapers, the front jacket, and as follows: photographs for A thyme bed (pages 18–21), A purple bed (pages 40–43) and A herb-lined pathway (pages 88–91) were all taken by Clive Nichols; page 8 right and page 30 below right were taken by Caroline Arber at Iden Croft Herbs, Staplehurst, Kent, UK (www.herbs-uk.com); page 9 below was taken by Caroline Arber at Bruisyard Vineyard & Herb Centre, Suffolk, UK (+44 (0)1728 638281).

index

acknowledgments

The author would like to thank the many people involved in making
this book, including Anne Ryland, Jacqui Small, and Marianne Majerus, whose
photographs make it so beautiful. Thank you to Caroline Davison for editing
the text so efficiently; Caroline Davison and Larraine Shamwana for their help
with photoshoots; Mark Latter for his stylish graphic design; John Powles and
The Romantic Garden Nursery for lending their topiary and herbs; Brian and
Rosemary Clifton-Sprigg for supplying many beautiful plants and allowing us
to photograph their excellent nursery; Jane Seabrook and The Chelsea
Gardener for lending plants and the use of their charming nursery setting.

Thanks are also due to the following people who lent their own beautiful
gardens as backdrops for photography: Mr and Mrs David Cargill,
Ethne Clarke, Mr and Mrs Robert Clarke, Viscount and Viscountess De L'Isle,
Major Charles Fenwick, Mrs Clive Hardcastle, Mr and Mrs Derek Howard,
The Lady Tollemache, Mr and Mrs Richard Winch. Thank you to
Peter Goodwins for building many of the projects, and to
Jill Hamer for typing the text.